A bright spot in the yard

A bright spot in the yard

Notes and stories from a prison journal
JEROME WASHINGTON

THE CROSSING PRESS / Trumansburg, New York 14886

Several paragraphs of Ted Howard's Introduction originally appeared in the *Ithaca Times,* July 21-27, 1979.

Cover design by Jason Wong
Front and back cover photographs by Jason Wong
Photograph of Jerome Washington on page viii by Steve Taylor
Book design by Martha J. Waters

Library of Congress Cataloging in Publication Data

Washington, Jerome, 1939-
   A bright spot in the yard.

   1. Attica Correctional Facility.   I. Title.
HV9481.N62A888   365'.44'0974793   81-12597
ISBN 0-89594-063-9   AACR2
ISBN 0-89594-064-7 (pbk.)

To my mother and Joyce.
My mother for obvious reasons,
Joyce for her friendship and support.

Table of Contents

Jerome Washington

Preface

There are two kinds of writers in prison: the ones who take exception to the system and the ones who appease the system. The French had their collaborators, and so does the American prison system.

The first is the writer who happens to be in prison in much the same way as a writer might happen to be in New York City, or the Antarctic, or any other geographical location against his will. He is still a writer, and he is obligated to affirm, through his craft, his differences with the prison system. There can never be an acceptable compromise between the repressive nature of prison and the writer's need for creative freedom.

It is this need which leads the writer-in-prison to unmask, at every turn, the arbitrary character of the system in which he is forced to live. That obligation is no less because he is in prison than it is for writers struggling against oppression elsewhere.

For most prisoners, the central concern is one of escaping the horrors of the system. For the writer the central concern is to reveal these horrors. To make his statement, he must sometimes use satire, humor or other oblique methods; seldom can he confront the system head-on. Often he must strip the facade, layer by layer, until the core is exposed. At other times the writer need only scratch the veneer to reveal the decay underneath.

While the revealing process continues, the writer must undergo a day-by-day catharsis by asking himself: "Am I doing the right thing?" Not to resolve this question is to run the risk of becoming that which every person is always in danger of becoming—an accomplice to the system, the kind of person who endangers others.

Unlike many writers in the "freer" outside world, the writer-in-prison cannot afford the luxury of writing to entertain the reader. In prison, where every free thought is contraband, writing is a serious, deadly business, and every word must count.

On the other hand, there is the "prison writer." He kowtows and blends with the system. He and his craft are subjugated by the system. Therefore, prison writers strengthen the very system which oppresses them. They are contented to "sing while they slave," and their prose and poetry only serves to restate, rather than incriminate, the misconceptions and stereotypes nurtured by the system. In short, they become as much a functioning part of the prison as are the guards, the officials and the administrators who pass the buck and protect themselves at the expense of their humanity. Such writers are accomplices in building prison walls, instead of conspirators in destroying them.

I feel that as a writer-in-prison, I have no alternative but to use the few tools I have to expose and indict the prison system. Of course, there are inherent dangers when any prisoner chooses to speak out. But the dangers of silence are far greater. One need not set out with the goal of indictment in mind. All one needs to do is to write as honestly as one can, and the indictment will stand clear.

Although my *Notes from a Prison Journal* are presented as non-fact, that does not mean that they are fiction. They are drawn from my experiences and observations during the seven years I have already spent in prison. Included in this grouping are episodes, vignettes and even thoughts which one prison official characterized as "venom." To me, that is by far the best review any writer-in-prison could ever hope to receive. I am extremely thankful to that official for the degree of his myopia and the level of his prison paranoia.

—Jerome Washington
transmitted from Attica Prison,
Attica, New York
September, 1979

Introduction

Jerome Washington is a remarkable writer not just for his artistry and skill with language but for his ability to report on his world from two perspectives, one familiar and one unfamiliar. He has lived among us as a teacher, soldier, businessman, political activist and journalist and can, when he chooses, employ the literary techniques used by most writers we are accustomed to reading. But he also knows the world of prison life from the inside, and can speak as one with those dispossessed people who have always lived in the dark hidden corners of society—not just in prisons but in ghettos, gangs, and marginal subcultures of crime.

I first met Washington in July of 1979 when I interviewed him for an Ithaca, New York, newspaper. In a bleak conference room at Attica Prison, where he is serving a fifteen-year-to-life sentence on a murder conviction, I met a man of forty, with bright almond-shaped eyes and a short afro. He was dressed in an orange sport-shirt and crisp dark slacks; he had a straightforward manner and an easy, sometimes mischievous smile.

"Prison education—never sit with your back to the door," he told me. I knew he was joking; I also knew that I wouldn't be comfortable until I changed the position of my chair, and did. The ice was broken. We started talking, and didn't stop for six hours. I forgot temporarily that I was inside a prison, for it became clear to me right away that I was talking with a colleague, someone who was a human being, a man, a writer first, and last and least a prisoner.

Jerome Washington was born in Trenton, New Jersey, in 1939, and spent what he describes as a normal childhood "collecting snakes and swimming at the swimming hole." When he was twelve, his aunt sold her house and gave him 400 books, and he set out to read them all, starting with Plato and Shakespeare. He attended Columbia University and then served in the Army for three years in Vietnam and in Europe. After his discharge, he stayed in Europe for several years. Back in New York, he became involved with the civil rights and peace movements. He went on voter registration drives to the South with SNCC, helped organize peace rallies for the National Mobilization Against the War in Vietnam, was at Resurrection City in Washington during the Poor People's March. Like many 60's dissidents, he is sure he acquired an extensive FBI file during this period.

Jerome Washington has fought successfully to keep his mind alive in prison. If anything, the pressures of prison life have forced it to work overtime. While at Auburn Prison, he founded and edited the *Auburn Collective,* which became the first prison newspaper in the state to gain national recognition, receiving ten awards for feature writing, news writing, and editing during Washington's tenure as editor from 1974-78. He has been an instructor in writers' workshops at both Auburn and Attica, and has worked with the Literacy Volunteers of America tutoring other prisoners. He has coordinated several Inside Circuit Lecture series, bringing writers and professors into prison educational programs. And he has kept writing continually. A full-length play has been produced in part by the Kuumba Repertory of Ithaca College and by The Family in New York City. He has written many shorter plays, some of which have been broadcast on radio, and his short stories, articles, book reviews and poems have appeared in *The Transatlantic Review, Yardbird Reader, Dodeca, Contact II, CORE, The Communicator,* and in the newspapers of Syracuse, Rochester, Buffalo, and Ithaca, New York. He has also written two novels.

Washington's view of life behind bars is uncompromising and powerful. Like the best writers who have been in prison— Dostoevski, Dickens, Solzhenitsyn come to mind—Washington not only shows us the raw pain and loneliness that prisoners experience, but makes us understand how the entire social system works to produce this human wretchedness. There is also a great deal of poetry and humor in Washington's writings, and a continual theme of the survival of the human spirit through small heroic acts of self-assertion.

Approaching Attica Prison, where Jerome Washington lives, and where, ten years ago, 11 hostages and 32 inmates were killed by corrections officers and state police during the famous riots, you see the high grey wall of the prison loom up before you like a cement fogbank half a mile long. Closer up, its pointy towers, flag-waving and turreted, resemble a child's toy fortress expanded to monstrous proportions. As you enter the place, you walk past heavy metal doors that crash and clank behind you, you pass through a metal detector, you present your identification papers, you have your personal property carefully inspected and returned to you by a uniformed official. You walk with other visitors toward the inner buildings of the enormous compound, huge brick and cement structures with barred windows and surrounding chain-link fences. At two check points, your documents are gone over again by officials. Finally, you are cleared for entry into the visitor's room.

Standing before the doorway, you have the distinct feeling

that you are entering a foreign country—one with its own customs officials and army, its own laws and ways of enforcing them.

On first view, the visiting room suddenly seems incongruous. Though you feel as if you had left United States soil, the place looks like the waiting room of a very large American bus terminal, with coke and food machines along the wall, formica tables and plastic chairs set out in rows. Seated at the tables are the same people you'd see at the bus station: Mom and Pop, the wife and kids—black, brown and white: an ordinary American scene.

This sense of disorientation will never leave you while you are in the visiting area. You will never know what country you are in until you have learned what goes on behind the visiting room's walls. This you will not find out from the government of this place, for it does not want you to know. But if you listen carefully to the characters in the few really good books—like Jerome Washington's—that have been written by the citizens of places like this, then, after some further disorientation, you may begin to discover where you are. And you may begin to understand that you have always been there.

The prison world of Jerome Washington's writings is a state in which the sole preoccupation of the government is total social control of its people. This control is both physical and psychological, and is so much a part of everyday minute-to-minute existence that the line between the two is almost invisible. It is a world in which people are killed and wounded in paramilitary operations disguised as law-enforcement exercises, where lips are cut, noses smashed, and prisoners have their jaws broken "against the boot of a guard sergeant" who reports that he was only trying to help the man to his feet. No wonder most of the prisoners wear earplugs in order to sleep, and wear psychological blinders in order to get through their waking hours.

In the story about New Year's Eve, the prisoners themselves, sexually deprived and in a state of perpetual rage against their keepers, take out their aggressions on each other, thereby helping the regime to maintain a reign of terror which is as effec-

tive a form of social control as any of its own operations.
While the "smooth-skinned boy of twenty-one" is being gang-raped, the guard stands by languidly smoking a cigarette.
When the men are finished with the boy, they are not punished for their act, for the institution knows that they are its unwitting accomplices. The boy himself, bleeding and inert in the prison hospital, is the only one charged with an offense; he is punished for " 'inciting a riot' with his own . . . smooth-skinned ass." Punished, that is, for being a victim—a metaphor for the process by which the state protects itself against so many victims by putting them in prison in the first place.

There is a "logic" to the boy's punishment. Victims are dangerous social elements—if they get angry, they might try and stop being victims and challenge the established order to do so. To side with the victimizers, as the guard does, is to play safe, for as long as they are free to hurt each other, they are not thinking—a dangerous activity—about their loss of freedom to do anything else. They are not challenging the order that keeps them from their freedom. In this world, the only "well-adjusted prisoner" is a violent prisoner, for he is acting according to the expectations of his society.

To do otherwise—to quietly, patiently gear one's life to the moment of one's release, like Cold Duck in another of Washington's stories, is to challenge the way things are done. That Cold Duck is able to resist all the guard's efforts to make him lose his temper is a defeat for the authorities, an admission that the institution cannot force every prisoner to adjust to its expectations.

Prisons are supposed to rehabilitate people. Every prisoner knows this. Every prisoner also knows—as the guard in another story says—that "rehabilitation is a hoax." But the fact that prisons do maintain a certain number of rehabilitational and educational programs to justify their existence makes for a dissonance of perception in every prisoner's mind which constitutes in itself an effective means of psychological control. There is always the expectation and the hope that prison will help a prisoner in some way, will at least take care of his basic human needs for food, shelter, and medical attention. When these needs are only partially met, the prisoner finds himself in a state of permanent tension which he cannot release against the authorities for fear that other basic needs will be denied him. Offering, then threatening to withhold; promising, then keeping only fractions of promises—the technique works, keeping everyone in a crippled state of uncertainty.

In one story, Long Tongue, a jazz musician, provides a true remedy for the prisoners. "The blues is our antidote, and Long Tongue, the Blues Merchant, is our doctor," Washington says of him. With his performance, the musician touches every member of his audience personally; he empathizes with their sufferings and longings and reminds them of the beauty and strength of their souls. (Except perhaps for Baldwin's story, "Sonny's Blues," I can recall no better literary description of jazz music's effect on an audience.) *This* is rehabilitation, but its message is smuggled contraband.

The authorities cannot prevent Long Tongue's message from reaching the prisoners, they can only prevent it from infecting one of their own—a guard who has relaxed his surveillance for a moment and has begun to respond to the music. He is told, in a glance from his superior, "You get paid to watch, not be human." Then "The guard jerks himself up and looks meaner than ever." The system here cannot brutalize its civilian citizens—for the moment, they are out of its reach—but it can, as it must, continue to brutalize those who control the civilians.

It becomes clear in Washington's writings that the system can never completely succeed in controlling and dehumanizing its subjects. His characters have dreams of better lives than those of violence and repression. Despite their environment, they keep their dreams alive. Perhaps because of it—because in prison, they often have nothing else left except dreams.

In "A Woman on My Wall," a prisoner experiences a sensual love and visions of idyllic landscapes in a fantasy in which he communicates with a woman who is more real to him than the walls of his cell. In "Cleanhead" and "Shing-a-Ling," both humorous pieces, we meet prisoners who dream of improving themselves. In the first story, Cleanhead discovers the ultimate con—a Dale Carnegie course—and plots to apply it to his profession of crime. Shing-a-Ling is motivated to teach himself to read and write first by his love for a fellow prisoner, and then by his need never again to be made love's victim; he understands, after being rejected, that he must find something real in his life—literacy—to replace the illusions about himself which he has been using to convince others that he is a slick operator.

In the title story, "A Bright Spot in the Yard," we see a comradeship develop between a new prisoner and an old one, the latter a man whom everyone else considers mad because he spends his days smiling up at the sky. Other men, who supposedly have a grip on reality, shake their heads sadly as they pass by him. At first, even the young prisoner is afraid of him, and keeps a piece of pipe ready in his back pocket in case the older man should attack him. Fear and distrust are the norms here, for in a world controlled by routine brutality, paranoia seems to equal sanity. But in this story, it is the "sane" characters, the men who place their faith in the conviction that the tangible, the hard, the brutal, the slick are reality, who are broken; they are the ones who are reduced to mumbling, shuffling wrecks. The young prisoner, who has not lost his willingness to trust others, is allowed to share the "insane" world of his mentor. He discovers a world of beauty in his imaginative fantasies, a "bright spot" far removed and far superior to the prison yard where he is standing. His mentor survives prison and is released, and the young man, like an apprentice artist, is entrusted to pass his knowledge on one day to another younger prisoner.

The prison world of Jerome Washington is a totalitarian state where, because they allow men to remain strong, "dreams are contraband." Dreams interfere with the message that the authorities broadcast to their subjects a thousand times a day: that prisoners are not human and need not, must not be treated like humans. But the fact that the "Bright Spot" prisoners have found a more powerful message to live by—and the fact that Washington has filled his book with humor, insight, and beauty—belies the message, and exposes it for what it is: an illusion more insane than the spaciest of prisoner fantasies.

True insanity, then, is the process by which a prison attempts to turn a human being into a thing, often creating "a walking time bomb, a lethal weapon aimed at society." Violent repression, which quickly spreads the word to its victims that violence is the only means of solving problems, may make the prisoners hate the world, but that hate is clearly a human attribute, a natural and sane response to a brutal environment. And while it is one response, another, Washington makes clear, is a desperate insistence on nurturing and protecting those other human attributes—the ability to experience love, beauty, hope—that are all a prisoner has to define himself as valuable, as sane, as human.

The totalitarian landscape of Jerome Washington's writings reminds me of similar places I read about frequently, places like El Salvador, South Africa, the Soviet Union. I think that when Americans read about random terror, arbitrary torture, secret penal archipelagos in these countries, we are incensed, but are also somewhat reassured that they aren't happening here; we can dismiss reports of atrocities with the thought: What can you expect from banana republics, white minority enclaves, communist dictatorships?

And when we enter a prison as a visitor, it is initially reassuring to feel a little like a tourist, to experience the place as a foreign country with its own laws and customs. If all the people in the visiting room were speaking Spanish or Zulu or Russian, we might be even more reassured.

The problem is, of course, that they are not. They are speaking American English. They look and act just like us, and often we cannot tell which are the prisoners and which are the visitors.

In fact, as Jerome's characters make clear, they *are* us. And the illusion that part of America is foreign is just that: an illusion—as surely an illusion as the belief that repression equals rehabilitation, that power equals justice, that incarcerated people equal non-humans capable only of sociopathic acts.

Our perception of prison as a foreign state is not necessarily a result of any cowardly need we have to be reassured about the people we see there. The illusion that there are *us* and there are *them,* that prisoners belong in a mental category labelled *the other*—this illusion has been erected for us, intentionally. It is, and is supposed to be, as formidable a barrier to our understanding of how our society works as the high prison walls are a barrier to our access to the life that goes on behind them.

In order to kill, or repress, or even to hurt another human being, those in command must first view him not as a human being but as a faceless enemy, a thing, a mere category—*the other*—a life-force capable of any random menace to *us*. This, Washington makes clear, is what prisons attempt to do. And this, Washington makes equally clear, is impossible to accomplish. The best a prison can do is maintain the illusion that it can be done—a lie that all too often convinces and even sometimes seduces us into a false sense of reassurance. But as we read about the lives of Washington's people—who have unmistakably succeeded in keeping their humanity intact—we begin to realize that prison walls, like the illusion they defend, have been erected as much to keep us *out* as to keep people in.

How is it that we have allowed our society to create such institutions as prisons, where the kinds of cruel and inhuman treatment we condemn in other countries go on daily on American soil? I believe that it is because we are used to tolerating prison-like places—ghettos, barrios, Indian reservations, Appalachian coal company hamlets . . . and not just geographically defined areas, but mental asylums, hospitals, schools, segregated neighborhoods . . . segregated minds. I think we are used to considering these places as the only appropriate locations for *them,* those people we cannot or will not deal with or accept. I think we are used to swallowing the illusion that the authorities—"the government," "the experts," "the free enterprise system"—know what is best for certain *others* who worry or threaten us, and that we need not concern ourselves about them, or apply our "normal" moral criteria to the ways in which they are treated.

There is, of course, nothing reassuring about this illusion. Closing our minds against oppressed people does not make them go away, does not solve their problems, does not reconcile them to our neglect; as we know, it can turn them into "lethal weapons aimed at society."

But even worse, swallowing the illusion can turn us into accomplices in the destruction of our own abilities to see, to feel, to empathize, to be as human as we need to be. We are the ultimate victims of the prison lie—it imprisons our minds.

To understand this—as Jerome Washington's writings help us to do—is a step towards freeing our minds.

By keeping his own mind free and strong—by keeping his artistry alive—he is allowing us to do the same. For his characters, by coming alive to us, have survived their physical and mental prison, and we can share in the triumph of their humanness over repression. Sometimes their humanness is brutal and sad, sometimes it is warm, inventive, humorous, even beautiful. It is, in short, much like our own. For showing us this, Jerome Washington deserves not only our admiration, but our gratitude.

—Edward Hower

(Hower, novelist and journalist, teaches at Ithaca College in Ithaca, New York)

Notes
and Stories
from a
Prison Journal

Notes

When The Man takes your name and gives you a number, the first thing you have to adjust to is not who you are but how many digits you have become.

■

Next to the flagpole, in front of Attica Prison, is a granite monument. On the monument, in alphabetical order, are the names of the eleven civilians and prison guards who were slaughtered in the riot of '71. They were picked off by their fellow guards, co-workers, Attica neighbors, and lifelong friends when Rockefeller ordered the prison yard to be retaken. The monument symbolizes the collective guilt shared by the living.

Altogether 43 were killed that day. But, as if no prisoners ever lived, therefore never died, none of the dead prisoners' names are memorialized in the granite.

Each morning a trusted prisoner strolls out to raise the flag. Each evening he returns to lower the flag. Inbetween he sits in his cell. Inbetween he doesn't exist.

■

"Attica! The name rattles my teeth like snakes," a West Coast friend wrote.

"The myth is the real prison," I wrote back. "It's thicker than the walls. The officials and the guards as well as the prisoners are locked in by the myth like pieces of a complicated Chinese puzzle."

As with the ancients whose mythology precluded everything except that which was preordained by the Gods, at Attica everything is held in check by a mythology of security. The mythology is translated into a "what if" philosophy and the chief of security is the philosopher.

■

Those of us who are in prison have been convicted. Everyone else is still on trial.

■

The next morning they told us that the screams had come from a prisoner who couldn't cope, and had gone berserk in his cell. They went on to explain that the blood splattered on the basement wall had come when the prisoner had slipped, headlong, down the stairs, and had cut his lip, and smashed his nose, and broken his jaw against the boot of the guard sergeant who had tried to help him up.

We nodded, and thanked them for the information and their time. That night we slept with earplugs.

■

"I'm not sophisticated," Hammerhead said, as he straightened his jockey shorts and scratched his balls, "but I am for real."

We all agreed that that was more than could be said for most people, including some of us who stood around like penguins on an iceberg, agreeing with Hammerhead.

■

Everything is a shade of grey. That's the color of prison.

The sky is grey. The walls are sand-grey. The yard is grey-black asphalt, and the inmates' uniforms, which appear green, are really a shade of grey.

Grey as a color is neutral; as a controlling force it is repressive; and debilitating as a life influence.

Grey controls all. It gets into the mood, the spirit, and even the food has a grey-bland taste.

It is no accident that grey is the chosen color. An integral part of any controller's plan is the color scheme.

In prison, grey dominates.

■

Prisons are abnormal places. Where else can a 145 pound man call a 250 pound giant a "punk?" He gets away with it because he is a guard, with guns on his side and the other is an inmate in a cage. After a few months of displacing aggressions and stuffing emotions, every inmate becomes a walking time bomb, a lethal weapon aimed at society.

■

Andy

Andy was one of the nicest young guys in the joint. He was quiet; he minded his own business and stayed mostly to himself. That's the criteria for being a good con.

When most prisoners went to the yard for baseball, chess and other recreational games, Andy stayed locked in his cell. He was waiting for his mother to come visit. She never did. Still, he kept his only dress shirt clean and neatly pressed, and he kept his hope alive.

In the yard one Monday morning, Andy spotted a new arrival, a transfer from another prison. He and the new man were not friends but they came from the same ghetto neighborhood. That's not much, but in prison it is more than enough for an alliance. They greeted each other as "home boy."

Each weekend the other man would disappear into the visiting room and on Monday he would tell Andy everything, including the kinds of vending machine sandwiches he and his visitor ate for lunch.

Finally, after some months, Andy confided, "I'm going to have a visit, too. Soon as my mom saves the money to come, she's going to make the trip to the prison and visit me."

Andy repeated this sad line until the other man stopped relating the Monday morning memories of his Sunday visitor. Slowly, the man put a distance between Andy and himself. And when they would chance to come face to face, he would never look Andy in the eyes.

"Did I hurt you in some way?" Andy asked politely. "Why are you avoiding me?"

The man kept his eyes lowered and tactfully tried to evade the truth.

Andy pressed for an answer. The man had no choice.

"I feel bad telling you." The man stumbled through his words. "God help me. I can't lie. Your mother isn't coming to visit you. All along, every week, she's been visiting a guy in Cell Block Two. She brings him food and clothes and even puts money into his account."

Andy had stopped listening. The gloom settled over him, the captain of a sunken ship. His mother visited a man who was locked in a cell not fifty yards away yet she would not come to see her son.

The man finished his truth by saying, "I'm sorry to be the one to tell you. Really I am." Then, "God bless you," he said as he walked away.

For the next two weeks Andy didn't speak to anyone, not even himself. Then one Sunday morning, Andy put on his clean, neatly pressed dress shirt and walked up to a guard. The guard, one of the few humane guards in the prison, greeted Andy with "Good morning." Andy answered by screaming obscenities in the guard's face. The guard tried to recover but Andy didn't give him the chance.

Andy's fist slammed into the guard's face. The second blow took the guard to the floor.

Fellow guards rushed to the rescue. They beat Andy until Andy begged to die. Then they left the blood for other prisoners to see and mop away.

The injured guard did not understand and the other guards never asked why Andy had picked him to slug. No one cared; no one wanted to know.

Least of all to care about her son was Andy's mother. She heard the story of his near death beating on her weekly trip to the prison to visit the other man. The man mentioned it as an afterthought; she received it as conversation in passing.

■

Notes

Every prison has a "Shorty," a "Heavy," a few "Slims,"
a couple of "Chicos," one or more guys calling themselves
"Brother," and an assortment of "Juniors" and "Youngbloods."

The same names recur from prison to prison like set moves
in a game of chess. Each has a story behind it. Each has a
reason and logic for being.

Hard Luck Henry was busted on Friday the 13th by an off
duty cop. Bitedown bit his lover's cock off. Boxhead Mike's
name speaks for itself. Wizard can make wine out of Kool Aid.
If push comes to shove, he can get high on mess hall soup and
a long conversation. Waco is as wild as a cowboy playing hop-
scotch. He hasn't cooled down yet. Loco Larry is a space
case and Pop is the oldest man in the cell block.

Every name fits, including Conjugal John. Hook, crook, beg
or pay, John has fucked every homo in the prison.

■

For those who can't imagine what it's like to be in a cell, lock yourself in a closet. Think of all the things you enjoy most in life. Now reach out and ask yourself: "Where are they?"

■

Turning the corner into the prison yard for the first time is like stepping onto the set of a Cecil B. DeMille spectacular where most of the extras are black.

Everyone has a yard image. Still there are no plush trimmings, trumpet fanfares or superstars. The only Herculean act performed is survival.

I scan the yard for a friendly face. There is none, yet one is familiar. He doesn't recognize me so I don't speak. But the next time I see him strolling the avenue, flashing fake diamonds and draped in dyed rabbit, he'll not convince me that he was vacationing in Miami or Vegas. I know where he has disappeared to. I am here also.

The thirty-foot high walls tell me that yesterday was a better day.

■

At noon today we waited an extra half hour to get into the Mess Hall. It was so nice to be free from the steel cells that, at first, no one minded the wait. There was a lot of bullshitting, joking, sap-rapping and high-jiving—the kinds of trivia inmates get into to relieve the tensions.

Then the rumors started. They came like birds in the night, and no one could pinpoint their origin.

The first rumor attributed the delay to Muslim inmates in the mess crew. The scheduled meal was ham and even handling swine, to them, is a sin, so they were refusing to serve it; thus they would save us from ourselves. The words rushed from mouth to ear to mouth, like falling dominoes the rumor went through the chow line. Before the word had reached the terminal of the last ear, a new message was on the drum.

Now the rumor spread that a rat had been found stewing in the wax beans, and for the vegetarians, this is a no-no. Next it came that soap powder had been used instead of cornstarch to thicken the gravy. Another told of a mouse committing suicide in the chocolate pudding. Each rumor sounded truer than the one before. They were all conceivable. We had little doubt that, in that kitchen, anything could happen.

Soon, like echoes, angry gripes followed the stream of rumors; the wake was alive with whispers of militant flotsam.

A nervous guard picked up the growing vexation, and finally a guard sergeant showed on the scene. Awkwardly, he explained that health inspectors were touring the Mess Hall, and that chow was being delayed until after their inspection.

We had no more reason to believe him than the other things we had heard. Yet, when we did get to eat it was with the feeling that for once it was safe.

■

"This won't take long," Captain Boss of the blue shirt mob said. "It'll be over and done long before you know, or even suspect whatever it is that we'll be doing to you is happening to be happening to you." He smiled like a part-time friend. "Don't fight back," he said, "or you'll break my club."

■

Cold Duck

Cold Duck had served twenty-two years behind the wall, and was soon to go free. That's all that mattered. He had geared his life to this point in time. Each tick of the clock was one less which he would have to stay here, and each step carried him closer to the street door. For the last five years, he had kept his nose clean. He had no rule infractions, not even a notice for an overdue book from the library. Now that there was a light at the end of his tunnel, Cold Duck dreamed about being free.

A hard-ass guard, fresh from the academy, out to make a cheap reputation, called Cold Duck a faggot. Cold Duck shook it off.

The guard smashed a matchstick house which had taken Cold Duck three years to build. Cold Duck swept up the pieces, and thought about his freedom.

Not even the angry tears which rushed into Cold Duck's eyes, when the guard implied that his dead mother had been a whore, could blot out the light in his tunnel. Cold Duck had waited too long to see that light. Now nothing could turn it off.

The more hostile the guard became, the more passive Cold Duck reacted. At night Cold Duck prayed: "Please, Dear God, don't let me kill again."

On the morning of the day that Cold Duck was released, the guard stepped in front of him and blocked his path to the door. "It's too late now," Cold Duck smiled, as he looked past the guard, and to the outside world. "You're a defeated man."

The guard pulled himself straight, and mock pride covered his pasty face. He opened his mouth to speak, but Cold Duck cut him off.

"You've tried everything you know to break me," Cold Duck said, "but I won't give you reason to keep me here. I've beat you at your own game." Cold Duck's voice was a whisper, yet as cold as the steel cell he had survived. "Now the least that you can do is to stand aside and let a free man go free."

The guard wept. From that day on the guard was known as a punk.

∎

Notes

"It's not possible for you to be feeling that much pain."
Doctor Apathy leaned back in his chair and frowned up at me.

"I hurt all over," I said. "My stomach is burning up. I want
you to do something for me."

"Give this man a handkerchief," he said to his nurse. Then
to me, "wipe your tears before they drip on my magazine and
soil the playmate's navel."

■

Rehabilitation is a hoax," Tripe, the guard sergeant, stated.
"Don't waste your time on such trivia."

I was dumbfounded.

"A strong image is needed for rehabilitation to work," the
sergeant said, "I am the strongest here but I wouldn't want
anyone remade in my image."

I nodded in agreement, and received a seven day disciplinary
lockup for insulting an officer by assent.

■

Room number 1 in the prison hospital is called The Space
Station. It's the psycho-observation room. There is nothing
in this room except a mattress on the floor, a bare bulb in the
ceiling and ghosts of minds out of control.

Every night, from room number 1, shrieks and howls sound across the empty yard. They remind us, caged in the cells, that going over the wall is not the only escape.

As in a game of chance where every number is a potential winner, in prison every inmate is a potential space-case. We all have an inside story waiting to be screamed across the yard.

■

"So what if this food is unfit for canine consumption?" the Mess Sergeant said. "We ain't feeding dogs, we is feeding you." He gloated, then added, "The SPCA can't squawk about that."

■

"If you want to learn to crack a safe," the education officer said, "ask Pious Pete."

Pious Pete is the chaplain's inmate clerk. He looks two days older than water and has more time on the toilet than I have in prison. His record as a safe-cracker is listed in 15 states and two territories.

"Old Pete knows everything there is to know about cracking a safe," the officer said, then added, "but after pulling a job, he just doesn't know how to get away."

I thanked him for the information, turned and started off.

"Remember," he calls after me, "there ain't no get-away experts in prison. For that advice," he laughs, "best bet is to contact Nixon."

I made a mental note to do that and went off in search of Pious Pete.

■

My history is my cross. A deadweight. The mathematical certainties of one-plus-one, two-times-two, have more flexibility.

A gravestone will give arrival, departure, date, time, group and an occasional epitaph of atonement and/or wit.

But my history lives.

It crawls. It slouches. It slurps. It marches and dances and laughs, shouts. It trembles and treads. Runs. It is a child and can fly.

Sometimes my history stomps angrily in the vanguard, directing the patterns my future will take. More often my history is quiet, dormant, and lurking behind this circus clown's face I live.

■

"So I told the whore, 'Love me or leave me,' " Rock Candy explained as he rocked on the balls of his feet. "Now she's been gone six months and the only word I've got was a 'Get Well' card on Christmas Day."

■

"If you ever want to run a heavy con game on a victim," Crapgame explained, "you first have to let the vic think he's got the upper hand. When you've got him all fixed—mesmerized—he'll con himself. Then all you've got to do is lay in the cut, and count his bucks."

■

Leapfrog, standing in the chow line behind K.C. Lou, watched the food server flop sliced ham onto the trays of the inmates in front of them.

"Swine is bad for your health," Leapfrog said to K.C. Lou.

"No shit," said K.C., as the line moved one step forward.

"Sure," Leapfrog said. "The pig is a grafted animal. The cat-rat-dog. Scavenges its own shit. The abomination of all abominations. Save your life, don't eat the ham." He paused, then said, "best thing to do is to give yours to me."

"Fuck you," K.C. Lou retorted, "swine is divine; it's boss with hot sauce."

■

15

Prison is an oral place. There's not much to look at in a cell, so inmates do a lot of talking. Talking to your neighbor, or the guy locked five cells away, two above, or one below. And when no one else will give any rap, you talk to yourself.

Even in the yard, it's an oral place. Jiving. Joking. Shouting. Laughing. Crying. Often just plain lying. And when there's no one who will listen, you always have yourself.

Inmates will rap about anything, to anyone, to keep the tension off.

■

It's hell being locked in a cell, rehashing memories of what a woman looks like: no wonder Playboy does more business here than Harper's.

■

Summer comes strange to prison.

Spring passes along the handball courts, makes a U-turn below guardtower number twelve, then follows winter to the Death-house exit.

Summer yawns up: a cat stretching the sleep away. Not wanting pets, just to be left alone, it settles into a warm ball and waits the next move.

Autumn lurks in the wings.

■

"Hit a woman?" Ronnie Too-Sweet said. "Man, you have got to be crazy or smokin' dope. I once beat my girlfriend, and she ran off and joined the Marines. When she came home, she told me they had treated her worse than I ever did. But don't you know, in the meantime she had learned to fight."

■

Pop Rivers

Throughout the winter Pop Rivers spread bread crumbs for the pigeons. He found one sick and nursed it back to health. By spring the bird could have flown away; instead it followed Pop around the yard. Pop named the pigeon Henry and referred to it as his child. He fed Henry a special mixture of cereal and cookie crumbs and crushed potato chips. Sometimes Pop would give Henry a spoon of sugar, at other times a drink of milk. But Henry's favorite was the popcorn.

At night when Pop Rivers had to be locked in his cell, he'd put Henry in a cardboard box on a table in the yard. Pop always left the box open and Henry was free to leave but Pop's cell was never left open. In the morning when Pop came out for his walk Henry was always there.

When Pop came out on the morning of the summer's equinox, Henry was not in his box. He was on the table. The bird's head had been chopped off, his wings and legs severed from the body and Henry's heart had been cut out. All the parts had been arranged in a neat line and the blood was still sticky.

Pop Rivers and a few friends went to the guard captain and pleaded that an investigation be made. "Who murdered Henry while we inmates slept locked safely in our cells?" Pop cried.

"We don't plan to investigate," the captain snapped. "But if you insist, I'll give you thirty days in The Hole for violating the rules against having a pet in the first place."

Pop Rivers could do nothing but silently curse the captain and find a place for Henry's grave.

■

Notes

They packed Alexander's things this morning, and sent them to his folks. They did it after everyone else had gone to work or school or to other assigned places. When we returned to our cell block, Alexander's cell was empty and scrubbed down as if no one had recently lived there. But we all knew differently.

It's very hard to wash away memories of a man hanging from cold cell bars and kicking his life away at the end of a knotted bedsheet, dying before the guards could cut him down.

■

"Ain't nothing cryptic or subtle about this place," Moe Jones, the inmate clothing clerk, said as he issued my first prison uniform. "Everything is up front. Direct. To the point and for real."

I pulled on the pants he had given me. They were too short; and the shirt was too tight.

"Fits you like a dream," Moe said between puffs of cigar smoke. Then he issued me a king size sheet for my pint size bed. "You'll shrink to fit the clothes," Moe said. "As for the extra large sheet, that's in case you decide to hang yourself. There'll be plenty left to cover the body."

■

"I wonder what the world is doing out there," I mused as I stared at the top of the lone tree that showed over the prison wall.

"Whatever the world is doing," Peewee, a street-wise realist, reminded me, "the world is doing it without us."

Frankie Cool, who had just received a Dear John from his woman, said, "You've sure got that right."

The three of us went to sit under the guntower and forget about trees, the world and the authors of letters that begin with: "I will always love you, but I thought you ought to know..."

■

To remain human in prison, one must break the rules.

■

Under my bed are boxes of letters. Cancelled stamps from places I've never seen. Pen pals. Names with no faces. Words without sounds. My surrogate family in an envelope.

When Saladine refused to take Thorazine, the guards said that he was rebelling. When Saladine tightened his fist against the pain of fifteen years in prison, the guards said that he had given the Black Power salute. When Saladine went to the Parole Board and asked to be released, the guards labeled him a "malcontent." When Saladine exploded and sent three fellow prisoners to the hospital, the guards relaxed and called Saladine a "well-adjusted prisoner."

■

Chaka Khan shook her black booty in the face of the warden's wife and the guards never understand why we relate to

Aretha Franklin when she shouts, "Give me R-E-S-P-E-C-T."

Everytime the warden sees us snapping our fingers, he smiles and prides himself for keeping us happy. What he doesn't realize is that we snap our fingers to keep our balance when strutting through his bleached-out shit.

■

Yesterday the homos stopped turning tricks and organized for prison reform. By noon an asshole bandit—as aggressive homo-chasers are called—who was turned down by a prison queen, was knifed by a scared-eyed boy who was protecting his manhood from assault. And two guards were K.O.'d when a pussy-hungry weightlifter took their night sticks and went berserk.

The warden, panicked by the sudden violence, agreed on first request to allow TV's in the cells and other reforms if the homos would call off their strike and de-organize. Within an hour the prison was back to "normal" and the warden walked easy.

His only other alternative was to drop his pants and stop the violence himself.

■

Only in prisons, police stations and welfare lines do you see bilingual signs and directions posted. Everywhere else, everything is English only. It seems that Americans only recognize Spanish-speaking people when there is a need to control them.

■

After ten years of jerking off, Willie went home to his wife who had waited with memories of Willie's love. She had stayed in practice, of course, and knew what love making was all about. But Willie, after ten years of non-experience, could only see his wife as a substitute for his fist.

■

20

The last time we tried a hunger strike the warden stormed into the Mess Hall and ordered us to eat. When no one made a move to break our solidarity by eating, the warden dragged a large chalkboard into the middle of the Mess Hall.

"This is your last chance," the warden shouted as he held up a piece of chalk for all to see, then prepared to write. "If you men don't start eating right now," the warden screamed, "I'm going to write the names of every informer, snitch and rat in the prison."

Before the chalk touched the board nearly every plate was clean.

■

New-breed guards seldom beat with clubs. Modern penology is not that personal. The system does a number on the brain cavity that creates psychological cripples.

A wounded mind takes longer to heal; the scars last forever.

■

Little Danny Lomax took a knife to the hospital. It was buried in his chest.

Eyewitnesses said that Danny had slipped and fallen while cleaning his toenails.

The only fingerprints found on the knife were Danny's where he had tried to un-stick himself before giving up the ghost. But rules are rules and the official investigators had no choice except to charge Danny with "homicide of self" and "destroying State property." At the bottom of the "unusual incident" report, the investigator wrote: "Little Danny Lomax. Former prisoner. Released by sudden death."

■

Old Man Henry Carter

Old Man Henry Carter knew everybody. He had come to prison before rules were rules and no records of him were kept. He didn't even have a number, just a cell, a faded prison uniform, a place in the chow line and a plastic bucket for hot wash water at night.

Old Man Henry's motto was, "You put it out right and it'll come back right." He had a kind word and gentle smile for everyone. Even when the young bucks would stomp angrily past his cell and disturb his rest with shouts like militant rabble, Old Man Henry would smile and quietly remember the young-years it had taken him to get used to his manhood, too.

The warden created a job for Henry. The warden felt that having a job would give Henry a sense that he was earning his keep. Each day Henry swept a clean floor and delivered empty envelopes to people who smiled and called him a "good old boy." And though Old Man Henry never missed a day at work, he would tactfully say that he only worked to ease the warden's guilt.

Two fellow prisoners, members of the Chaplain's Aid Committee, took turns writing letters so that Old Man Henry would receive some mail at the mail call time. They even took turns helping Henry answer their letters so that he would have something going out as well as coming in. Publicly, Old Man Henry would say how nice it was to be in touch with the outside world. But in private, he would wink and thank God that he was able to help the two younger prisoners do their Christian duty.

When Old Man Henry died in his sleep one night, the doctor listed the case of death as PRISON. The prisoners walked softly and said no harsh words. The guards laid down their clubs for one day and the warden ordered steak served in the Mess Hall.

■

Notes

"This used to be a good joint," the electric gate guard said.

They had taken his keys and had refitted him with a push button control. The buttons were color coded so he wouldn't confuse the word "open" with "close" and let a prisoner go free.

"Back in the old days when Lefty Collins was a tough guy, and Shorty Dog would fight back, we had a real good place here." He emphasized "real good." Then lamented, "Now I almost feel shame when we gang up on one of these new-breed prisoners. They worry more about bouncing a basketball than keeping their manhood."

He pushed his buttons and remembered the simplicity of turning a key and said, "It just ain't no fun kicking a pacified ass."

■

New Year's Eve. A smooth-skinned boy of twenty-one was gang raped in the bathhouse.

The guard on duty puffed an extra long, mentholated and filtered cigarette and took his time responding to the screams that were soon gagged away with a bar of prison soap.

When the guard did arrive, the only culprit left to apprehend was the smooth-skinned boy of twenty-one. Blood trickled from the boy's ripped asshole and cum smeared his inner thighs like egg white. The stretcher gang arrived and the boy was rushed past the hospital and into a punishment cell.

After the guard had checked the correct spelling, he wrote his report. The boy was charged with 'attempting to incite a riot' with his twenty-one-year-old-smooth-skinned ass.

While the gang rapists boast and plot, the guard lights another cigarette and awaits the next infraction of his bathhouse rules.

■

In prison, memories become hope. And hope becomes an absolute trap. Yet, to do nothing is treacherous.

■

The Woman
on My Wall

"Do you have fantasies?" Her voice a wind chime, tinkles come from everywhere at once and fill my small chamber.

I finish my pre-bedtime chores and turn toward her.

Her full, cushiony lips are freshly moistened as roses are with dew and partially open in a smile.

"You do have fantasies, don't you?"

Her dark, almond-shaped eyes are wide with interest and follow as I move.

I sit on my cot and gaze back at her. My eyes follow the plush oval curve of high, firm breast tipped with erect nipples, her tapered waist, the smooth, slow roll of her stomach disappearing into the V of her thighs, thighs slightly parted and framing her pink blossomed vulva nestled in downy angel hair. Her high formed *mons veneris* captures my attention. Even her toes stir my libido.

She is my mandala.

She is my sanctuary.

We walk a wood path down a gentle slope toward an afternoon beach. The air smells of lilacs and violets and feels velvet against my skin. Birds chirping high in the canopy of leaves herald us as trumpets do prince and princess. Smooth, white, crystalline sand spreads before us, welcoming our footprints as lovers do each other's hand. At water's edge, we shed our garments and naked, save for sun rays and Eros' smile, hand in hand we ease into warm water.

We make love on a wave. Rejuvenated. We are washed ashore to lay side by side upon the sand. Nature kisses us with a breeze, sanctifying our union.

Later, after snacks of wine and cheese, fruit and nectar, we sprawl in each other's arms whispering secrets too dear to be spoken aloud, kissing and feeling the earth quake and move. Then we rejoin love-making.

By starlight we softly say how strange it is that people make war and we fall asleep feeling free and nice and natural things against our skins.

"Yes, I have fantasies," I admit to the woman smiling at me. "At one time, I had memories but they are all gone now."

"Are your fantasies of me?" Nightingales are shamed by her voice.

The night bell clangs, ringing to end another day. The uniformed guard halts before my cell door. He peers in through the bars.

"Sheetrock," the guard calls me by my tough prison nickname, "were you talking to yourself again?" His tone is as impersonal as the "thank you" of a meat market clerk.

I continue to stare at the enchantress before me.

"Were you talking to yourself again?" he repeats his question, this time a bit harsher for being ignored.

"Yes," I force myself to say, "I suppose I was talking to myself."

"Don't let it get to you," the guard says as he moves on along the corridor of cells, completing his nightly head count.

"Don't let it get to you," is the same thing he has said to me, every night, for the last five years.

The programmed routineness is debilitating and treacherous. It affects both the watcher and the watched.

Soon the lights will be turned off and another alone night will settle in. There is never a change, except that which occurs within my mind.

I lean across the narrow cell space and lightly kiss the mouth of the woman smiling out from the magazine centerfold pasted to my cell wall.

She is my confidante.

She is my escape.

"Yes," I say to her, "my fantasies are of you."

"Please tell them to me," she cajoles as I lay down to monologue myself to sleep.

The return of the prison-grey morning comes too soon.

■

Notes

Everyone passes the buck. Even when they know the currency is counterfeit and the account is bankrupt, they still pass the buck. No one will stand up or even sit down for anything. The standard official reply is: "I'll get back to you later." Of course, later keeps getting later, and later, and later and . . .

Nowhere is the civil service game of CYA—cover your ass—played better than in prison. If anyone asks questions or complains, they can always blame it on the prisoners.

Shit rolls downhill.

■

When Big Red The Greek arrived in prison, his first act was to cut off all outside contacts. This included his wife and his girl friend, and his woman and even his woman's woman.

Then Big Red The Greek sat down and waited to be released.

■

Everybody called Latamore a bug, a space case or just plain crazy. No one took him seriously. Especially when he told about the nuclear submarine that he was building in his cell and how he would flush himself down the john and escape to cruise the South China Sea with Peter Lorre and Doctor Fu Manchu. Or about the helicopter that was nearly complete and would lift him over the wall and into a harem of mink-cunted nymphs.

He was on everyone's pay-him-no-mind list. Still Latamore was as happy as a madame counting the take and often said, in a way of a caveat, that he would escape and we would be left behind—asleep.

On the morning of the day that they cut Latamore down from the bars and painted over the marks from his rubber heels where, like a salmon going upstream, he had kicked himself to freedom, the guard sergeant asked us if we had heard anything during the night. The best that any of us could do was to lower our eyes and testify that when Latamore had made good his solo escape to the South China Sea and a world of mink-cunted nymphs, the rest of us were having nightmares.

No one had the heart to mention that we all had separate escape plans of our own.

■

We watched Hardluck Henry being led away, across the yard, by four guards. He had just gotten busted for drinking jailhouse booze in the baseball dugout and they were taking him to The Hole.

"I've known Hardluck for a long, long time," Little Brother T said. "We go way back together. We were once running partners on the street, and it don't surprise me one bit that he got flagged with wine on his breath. That's one dude that's always into something or other. One time he called me at three o'clock in the morning from a pay phone booth and says that he's in a jam and wants me to hurry over and pick him up. When I got on the scene he was in the phone booth, buck-ass-naked. He had one shoe and his hat in his hand. He said that he was screwing some woman and her husband came home and he had to jump out of the window and run."

We all laughed.

"You know something?" Little Brother T said with a straight face. "I never did ask him where he got the dime for the phone call."

■

"You ain't got to tell me about pain," Old Man Fish grunted. "I've been here for twenty-three years and you don't know what hurting is until you try acting as if it doesn't hurt."

■

Orangutan Jones

The first sign that Orangutan Jones was losing his grip came when he removed his woman's photo from the wall of his cell. It was an eight-by-ten, full-color blowup from a snapshot of a good time they had once on a North Shore beach. She had it especially made into a calendar and had written on it: "With each day you mark off, we'll be coming closer together. All my love, until the end." She had written that last year and the end came shortly after.

Orangutan Jones treasured that photo and often stated that it brought good memories. "Sometimes," he said, "when I look at it, I forget that I'm here in prison at all." Now it was gone from his wall and only the gummy marks of the masking tape which had held it there remained.

"It's the small things that get to me," Orangutan said as we walked the exercise yard. "Bit by bit, like Chinese water torture. At first I told myself not to take it personal." He ripped up the photo and a number of her letters—the latest was five months old—and dropped them into a trash can. "All it takes is a small show of love and a little reassurance from the outside for a guy to make it in here. And she couldn't even give that—a lie would have been better than the nothing she gave."

Three days later the guards found him sitting in the middle of the basketball court. He was bouncing a ball, crying and babbling to himself. They thought it was delirium brought on by jailhouse booze but to me the meaning was clear.

That night I lay awake rehearing Orangutan Jones as they led him to the observation room. "I want to thank you, baby," he said, "for all the little things you didn't do for me."

When dawn came, I was still wondering if I'd be the next to say those words.

■

Notes

The Warden asks, "How are you?" The guard sergeant orders, "Cop out," and the shrink drugs those who don't. The doctor issues an aspirin for everything and signs the death certificate with a grin. The preacher prays with half a lip and hangs onto his club. The prisoners ease their frustrations by sending each other to the grave.

■

"I ain't standing for no shit," Steel Bill shouted through the bars of his cell. He slammed his metal cell stool against the walls, bent the legs across his knee, then went on to add, "and I don't want no shit."

The word spread through the joint that Steel Bill had finally bugged out. It started as a whisper and grew into a warning shout. Steel Bill knocked out two guys for staring at his back and sent another to the hospital for crossing his path.

All night long Steel Bill shouted, "Give out, but don't give up!" Even the niggers who usually are quick to mock another's pain remained silent that night.

■

Each day I feed the birds outside my window. Since I am never sure if the birds that come today are the same that came yesterday, I limit my conversation to a few "hellos," and a casual "hi, there."

Extended conversations are impossible when no continuum can be identified.

Still, each day the birds come to pimp me for their bread. And each day I pimp them for their companionship. We pimp each other for survival.

Isn't that also a law of Nature?
∎

They stood around, goading Junior on like ranch hands cheering a bronc buster.

"Don't take no shit from The Man," one said.

Another added, "Your manhood is at stake."

Junior, whose flanks had never known the warmth of a woman's thighs, whose youth was still in his voice, swung at a uniformed guard and was dragged off, feet first, to be gang stomped in the privacy of the guardhouse.

After Junior was gone and the blood had been washed away, they stood around like overfed vultures, burping that Junior was a sucker for listening to them. All the same they kept an eye out for another hunk of young pigmeat to throw against the guards.
∎

Other than a miserly bit of grey sky, the only thing I can see over the prison wall are the tops of a few trees. I don't know what kinds of trees they are. I don't even care. They live and that is all that matters to me.

Year in, year out, we keep each other company. They are orphaned and outcast also. Their wood is too useless to harvest. They stand in place and rot. Except for the breath in my lungs, the trees are perhaps the most important things in life.

One tree is friendlier than the others. Its branches spread wide, welcoming arms, inviting birds to rest. Another is not friendly at all. Stark and bare like my cell it is the Scrooge of the lot—the nemesis of life. Not even leaves stay for long on its branches; even the wind slacks away. A thin tree, a late bloomer, stands alone off to one side, a rejected child still hoping to play. The last was struck by lightning. Its topmost branch is split like the fork in a country road. This one is my favorite, an extension of myself. In spite of the lightning blows, we survive—mutilated but struggling up the beach nonetheless.

■

Halftrack found her name in a sleazy, third-rate pulp magazine. She was looking for a pen pal, and so was he. Via the U.S. mail, they fell in love and vowed to write every day.

When his long distance lover finally came to visit, she turned out to be a *he* dressed as a *she*. Now Halftrack vows to blow up the post office.

■

There is a volume of love poetry in the prison library. I've memorized it page by page and can recite it word for word. Now I need someone who will listen.

■

A Bright Spot
in the Yard

Jomo was laughing to himself when I first saw him standing with his back pressed against the brick building at one side of the exercise yard. His clean-shaven head was tilted back on his short neck, his moon face glistened with sweat and his eyes were fixed on a point in the sky, high above the prison's grey walls.

"Him's really a strange piece of God's work." Spokane Mack spoke through his straight-across-the-face mouth and nodded toward Jomo as he, Tankcar and myself walked the yard.

Tankcar hunched his huge shoulders and pulled down the corners of his lips in a way that made the razor scar on his cheek stand out in bold relief. "A bona fide nut," Tankcar said, emphasizing the word "nut." "Some guys never recover from the trauma of being arrested."

I looked at Jomo out of the corners of my eyes. His eyes were wide. Staring. Entranced. Columbus sighting the New World; Moses looking into the Promised Land. I rubbed my hand down across my chin, remembered I hadn't shaved in two days and asked, "What's his trip?"

"Too many years behind the walls," Spokane Mack said. "Now him's on everybody's pay-him-no-mind list."

"That's his spot in the yard," Tankcar informed me. "Nobody ever stands there but Jomo."

I said it was a damn shame the way prison could do a person and vowed never to let it happen to me.

"Anybody's number can play," Tankcar reminded me.

As days eased into weeks and weeks into months, Jomo became more of an accepted fixture in the yard than a fellow prisoner, sort of like the guardposts. He'd be there on his spot when I'd come out into the yard and he'd be the last one to leave when we were ordered back to our cells at night. Sometimes I wondered about him, and a few times even felt sorrow, but like other prisoners, I had my own problems and seldom paid him any attention until the day he materialized at my elbow and asked for a match.

I handed him a book of matches.

He stared at the matches.

"Is there anything wrong?"

He turned his eyes on me. "Where's the cigarette?" he asked, then smiled.

It was the kind of smile that went all the way around his neck and showed a lot of pretty teeth. His eyes were glossy, but not fixed in a crazed stare. Still I stepped back, put a little more space between us and rested my hand on the eight inch length of steel pipe I had rolled into a magazine and tucked into my hip pocket. In prison, where paranoia and violence determines the life style, I intended not to be a victim—especially of someone who everybody knew to be a nut.

I kept my eyes on him. "What cigarette?" I asked.

His smile didn't change. "The one that you are about to give me," he said, then looked off into the sky as if searching for his next words. He found them and said, "I would look very, very silly striking a match with no cigarette to smoke." He smiled at me some more. "Now, wouldn't I?" he asked.

I studied his face for telltale signs of lunacy. I couldn't find any. He was just another guy dealing with prison life in the best way he could. There was nothing insane about that. I relaxed my grip on the steel pipe and handed him my pack of cigarettes.

He shook one free of the pack. "You're unlike the others here."

"How's that?"

He returned the pack of cigarettes and rolled the one he had kept between his fingers. His hands were large, had a lot of small scars on them. They were clean and the nails were trimmed close.

"You still trust." His tone told me that he was about to make his point. I waited. He hung the cigarette in his lips, lit it, blew a slow puff of smoke, then said, "This place hasn't burned the trust out of you yet."

"That's an awful lot to read into one cigarette," I said.

He smiled again. This time not as wide as before. Still it was a good smile, not a pasted-on deception. "If you didn't trust," he said, "you wouldn't have let me have your full pack."

I saw his point. I hadn't been in prison long enough to know all the ropes. I made a mental note to go along with the pipe in my back pocket.

"Actions tell the story." He blew more smoke and winked at me. Then, as an afterthought, he said, "As we get to know each other, I'll share my secrets with you."

"Secrets?" I leaned back a little and gave him one of those long looks that's meant to imply doubt.

"Yeah," he nodded. The sun bounced off his head as he moved it up and down. "Real secrets."

I gave him another doubtful look.

His face became serious. He caught my arm and pulled me closer.

I yanked free.

He leaned in on me and whispered, "I know how to escape this place."

I froze. I stared at him. My heart tried to pound a hole in my chest. Sweat rushed down my armpits. The words caught in my throat and I had to kick them out. "Escape? How?" The words trembled out like a knock-kneed school girl on her first date.

He smiled again. He knew that he had me. "In time," he whispered as he blew some smoke, then watched it drift away. "In time you'll get all the answers." Then he changed up, as if someone had called him from across the yard. "Right now, I have to go visit with a friend."

Jomo dropped the cigarette, crushed it out, turned on his heels and walked off. He kept his head high and rolled on the balls of his feet. A few guys saw him coming and moved out of his way. Instead of going into one of the cell blocks where his friend might be, he went directly across the yard to his spot and stood with his back to the building and turned his face to the sky.

I saw Jomo every day. Still, it was another two weeks before we spoke again.

I was coming from the Mess Hall when he fell in beside me and said, "To understand that some people don't understand is to be called insane."

I didn't bother asking him to explain. There was only one thing I wanted to know—how to escape.

"When you're ready," he said.

"Hell," I nearly shouted, "I'm ready to go now."

"You only think that you're ready." He turned and started away.

I called after him.

He stopped and looked back at me.

I took a step toward him, but he held up his hand, signaling me to a halt.

"I have a party invitation." He grinned. "And I never want to be late." He flicked a parting wave and crossed the yard to his spot against the brick building.

I was left standing in the middle of the yard like a man waiting for something to happen; nothing did. Jomo spent the rest of the afternoon standing on his spot in the yard and staring up.

The next morning I caught up with Jomo as he came from his cell block. He seemed depressed. His shoulders drooped and his head hung like a melon on a vine. The luster was gone from his face and his eyes were recessed and dull as if he hadn't slept. I spoke to him, but he rushed past and hurried on to his spot.

No sooner than Jomo braced his back against the building and turned his face to the sky, his depression started to lift. It was a transformation. His shoulders squared themselves. The deep-rooted smile returned, his face gleamed as if polished and his eyes became full and round and were alive with the excitement of a faithful worshipper witnessing a miracle. He started to giggle. Then he was laughing aloud. Tears came from his eyes and everyone who passed shook their head and gave him plenty of room.

"Why you hanging with that nut?" Tankcar asked as he and Spokane Mack eased up on me.

Tankcar's prison shirt was cut off at the sleeves and the seams were busted under the arms. His muscles were still pumped up and sweaty from working out on the weight pile. He was one of the best weightlifters in the joint. Spokane Mack rocked on his heels. He was cleaning his fingernails and chewing on a toothpick.

"The man ain't nuts," I said.

"Shit he ain't." Tankcar wiped a line of sweat from his face.

"Him's a space case," Spokane said, "look at him."

Jomo was hysterical with laughter. His eyes were riveted on a spot high in the sky, focused as if watching a comedy. He was a mesmerized child.

41

Spokane laughed and said, "Better watch yourself. That loony stuff is catching."

"Yeah, man," Tankcar put in, "you'd better check your role."

I looked over at Jomo. He was in his own world, his own space, his own time zone. He wasn't in prison, he wasn't anyplace, at least not any place that I knew anything about.

Spokane Mack put his nail file away, checked his nails to see how good a job he had done, then said, "In this place, it don't take much to end up like him is."

I thought about it for a moment, thought some more, then thought about escaping, then said, "I can handle it."

"Suit yourself," Tankcar said. He nodded to Spokane and said, "Come on. Let's walk."

They glanced at Jomo, then went on around the yard. I took the magazine from my hip pocket. The steel pipe felt heavy rolled in the magazine. I watched Jomo for a few seconds more. Then I went looking for a place to sit and read.

Jomo spent the next two hours staring into the sky and laughing to himself before coming over to where I sat reading. I was sitting on a small bench in the shade of the corner where two of the cell blocks came together. From there I had a full view of the yard. It was a three ring circus of inmates busy getting through another prison day.

A full tilt basketball game rushed up and down the asphalt court. Handball matches happened against one wall. Teams were being picked for volleyball. A softball game was warming up and men hunched at tables playing cards, chess and checkers. Off to one side, strong men worked in the flat sunlight, lifting iron weights. Runners, in tandems of five, jogged to a cadence called on every fourth step around the perimeter of the yard. Two homos lounged near the chapel door and guards kept watch while slick-kids and prison hustlers stalked their next victims. Only Jomo was alone and stood still.

Now he was standing before me, smiling.

"Some people will put anything into their heads," Jomo said as he looked down at me.

I slid over to make room for him.

"They'll fill their heads with shit," he said, "just to have something there." Then he asked for a cigarette.

I offered him the pack.

He smiled. "Still haven't changed?" he said and took one without taking the pack from my hand. He dug into his pants pocket, found a match, lit the cigarette, then apologized for ignoring me earlier.

"I had to clear my head." He leaned back and looked off into the sky. "The guy who locks in the cell next to mine. He thinks that prison is a game. He kept talking and yelling all night. I didn't sleep at all."

I agreed that one of the worst things about being in prison is not having a choice of who's around you.

Jomo puffed the cigarette and flicked the ash on the ground between his feet. "He's out of touch with himself," he said, "and because he doesn't realize the danger of this place, he's a danger to others."

I thought of all the prisoners who had been brutalized, and the ones who had died. "It takes all kinds," I said as I adjusted the steel pipe to keep it from sliding from under my shirt where I had it tucked. "We can't do each other's time here, but we can do it together."

On the basketball court an argument erupted over a doubtful score. A knot of angry inmates gathered under one basket and their voices got loud. The inmate referee rushed in and got the game moving again. The team managers were satisfied; the players were satisfied; the spectators were satisfied; and the guard in the guntower unloaded his weapon and replaced it in the rifle rack.

"Everyone here is a walking time bomb," I said.

"Some aren't," he said, "there's a few of us who have learned to keep our peace." He glanced sideways at me.

"It's the fucked up ones." I thought of a shit load of guys who made it their business to make life hard for others.

"That's what happened to me." Jomo dropped the cigarette butt and crushed it with the toe of his brogans. "My cell neighbor broke my peace last night. So, first thing this morn-

43

ing, I had to clean his crap from my head." He took a deep breath, then didn't say anything for a long time. When he spoke, he said, "I know that you understand."

I said that I understood the necessity of clearing his head but I didn't understand how he went about it. This led us into a conversation about interplanetary visitations and psychic phenomenon and telepathy and even how the uniformed grey of the prison is a well ordered scheme to neutralize and control us. We agreed that everything was possible, nothing could be discounted.

I slipped the steel pipe from under my shirt and rolled it back into the magazine, then slid the tight packet into my hip pocket. Jomo saw the pipe but said nothing.

Jomo tipped his head back and looked up at the sky. Puffy white clouds stacked on top of each other like cotton candy were moving in over the prison. He studied the clouds for a long time as if he was making something of them. Then he brought his head down and said, "I'll answer your questions."

How to escape was the only question I had but instead of asking that I asked why was he always watching the sky.

He laughed, but it really wasn't a laugh. It was more like a little chuckle that caused him to squint his eyes. "You're the first person to ever ask me that," he said. "Fact is, you're the first person in years to really talk with me."

From the way that others avoided him, I knew this to be true. Still I wanted to know his reasons for standing on that spot and looking at the sky, especially when he had said that he knew how to escape. So I asked him again.

He looked around to be sure that no one was close enough to overhear. Then he whispered, "The secret of that spot is dynamite."

"Hold it, Jomo," I said. "Don't take me on a trip. Just give it to me straight."

"This is straight." He nodded his head slowly up and down. "If it were known just how powerful the secret is, the guards would make that spot off limits and no one could go there ever again."

Perhaps everything I'd heard about Jomo was right. Perhaps

he was nuts after all. Perhaps I was a bit wacky, too, for believing he wasn't. But there was that outside chance that, crazy or not, Jomo did know how to get out of the prison. I had to take that chance.

"A secret place, huh?" I said, going along with him.

He nodded his head again.

I looked across the yard to his spot by the brick building. There was nothing there. Then I looked at the drab greyish-brown cell block buildings, then to the high sandy-grey wall with its peaked roof guntowers, then around the yard again and back to his spot. There was still nothing there. I could see nothing secret about it. It was just a little open space next to a prison building. On the contrary, if anything, it was conspicuous. It was at the most exposed point in the whole yard and I was sure that nothing covert could possibly happen there without every eye seeing it.

"What's so secret about being in the open?" I asked.

He hunched his shoulder, thought it over, then relaxed and said, "Some of the best kept secrets are in the open." His voice had an air of intrigue like a man making up riddles for others to solve. I could tell that he was having fun. "In the open," he went on, "no one ever bothers trying to find them."

A guard patrolling the yard ambled by. The guard tried to appear nonchalant but we knew his job was to watch and listen. We stopped talking until the guard had passed.

"Skeptics always fall the hardest. Come on." He bounced up from the bench and took me by the arm. "I'll show you." He pulled me.

I had to jog to keep from being dragged as he lead me past knots of talking inmates and across the yard.

"You won't need that pipe in your hind pocket anymore," Jomo said.

And I was suddenly aware of the weight of the pipe pulling my right hip down. It contrasted with the lightness of Jomo's hand on my arm.

"After today," he said as a group of four inmates got out of our way, "no one will bother with you again." He chuckled and added, "They probably won't even talk to you."

The four inmates eyed us as if we were contagious. I looked at them. Each turned his eyes away as if afraid that I would speak to him. I dropped the pipe, still wrapped in the magazine, into a garbage can as Jomo hurried me past and we came to his spot in the yard.

"I've never brought anyone here," Jomo said as we stopped. "Before I show you anything, you'll have to swear not to tell a soul until the right time."

He looked me in the eyes, then studied my face. He was as careful as a lockpicker. I felt that each pore in my skin was being scrutinized under a magnifying glass.

I mouthed a promise without the slightest thought that one day I'd be bound to keep and protect it.

"I got this spot from an old con everybody called Crazy Billy." His voice was low, as smooth as a golfer's stroke and each word was clearly spoken as if he was passing on something that should be remembered. "That was years back. This was his spot. He was always here and everybody thought that he was really crazy. But he wasn't and Crazy Billy knew that I knew he wasn't crazy. He just had another way of seeing things, that's all. When the time was right, Crazy Billy brought me here and showed me this spot."

The guard, making his rounds of the yard, slowed, glanced at us, and walked on.

After the guard was out of earshot, I asked what happened to Crazy Billy.

"Gone."

"Escaped?"

"No," Jomo said, then chuckled. It was the kind of chuckle you get when a person is enjoying an inside joke and you're left standing flatfooted and wondering what it's all about. "Crazy Billy escaped every day," he said, "but when it came time to leave, they released him."

He was inventing riddles again, words with double meanings. I didn't even try to understand.

"From this spot," Jomo said, "the prison disappears."

I was just as confused as before but this time I let out a

somewhat doubtful "What?" I looked at the ground, then surveyed the yard. Nothing had changed. Everything was just as it always had been. A prison.

Jomo was grinning. He was very pleased with himself. After he had checked to be sure that no one was nearby, he explained. "This is the only spot where you can stand and see nothing of the prison at all."

Around the yard the cell blocks with rusting window bars were still there. The watchposts and the uniformed guards were still there. The games inmates played were still going on. The sound of a thousand voices was still there. The lowered heads, the hollowed eyes and the shuffling feet were all still there. There was no doubt about it. This was still a prison.

"On this spot." Jomo stopped grinning and his face became solemn. His voice was low and filled with the inner warmth of a priest saying vespers. "You can become a wizard. A sorcerer. You can conjure the spirits of other worlds." His eyes were glossy and went into a far-off fix. "You can visit the infinite. Create passionate and hypnotic unions with the angels. Have affairs with queens, nymphs, concubines and common whores."

He was mesmerized and his words came in a flock, rushing together. He became absorbed in his own rhythm. "You can know the charm of the occult. Wall in the supernatural and make real anything you wish." His rhythm suddenly broke and the words came as a flash flood, then went into a long stammer. "Be sanctified. Supreme. Ubiquitous. Omnipotent. Almighty. Divine. Swifter than Mercury. More powerful than Paris, Mars, Apollo, the Titans and even Zeus."

He went on talking but I had stopped listening. My hope for an escape had become the charade of a lunatic. I felt sorry for him. I felt sorry for myself. I shook my head and started off.

"You can't leave," Jomo shouted. He grabbed my arm. His eyes were aflame, his jaw was set and his moon face shifted between panic and anger.

"Jomo," I said calmly, facing him square on and trying not

to show my disappointment; "You said you'd show me how to to escape. Now you're serving me word games."

"You'll be a god," he said.

"I'd rather be free."

I took a step to leave.

He slid his hand down to my wrist. I tried to pull away but his fingers were like vise grips and my whole arm ached from the pressure. With his other hand he caught the front of my shirt. His energy exploded. He lifted me, yanked me around and slammed my back against the brick building. I was stunned. I thought about the steel pipe in the garbage can. It was only a few yards away. I braced my foot against the wall behind me and pushed. But nothing happened. He was planted like Gibraltar at the Straits. I thought of all the stories about lunatics and their superhuman strength and looked around for help.

"You will be free." Jomo's mouth was close to my ear. He bit each word off so that it came hard and evenly spaced.

Out of the corner of my eye I caught a glimpse of the guard starting toward us.

Jomo released my wrist and brought that hand up under my chin. He forced my head up, high, then back hard until my eyes were on the sky.

The Sky.

Jomo was right. The prison had disappeared.

It was only when I was able to turn or lower my head slightly against the pressure of Jomo's hand that the prison came into view. Otherwise, there was only the open sky, dotted with fluffy, slow moving clouds riding eastbound zephyrs. The guard never came. There was no reason for him to come now. I relaxed and the weight of the prison was gone. I was a caterpiller suddenly transformed into a butterfly.

Jomo felt the change in me and relaxed his grip but didn't take his hands away. "Because you've been looking for the devious," he whispered into my ear, "you've failed to see the obvious."

I felt the smile forming. It came from a long time ago. From the other side of grief and sorrow. From my youth. From innocence. From the days when I had nothing to worry about. The smile struggled up through years of knotted guts, releasing tensions and relieving the pall and paranoia of prison as it came. Then It was there, spreading my lips back tight across my teeth, taking root in my face and feeling as if it was the only way ever to feel.

"Your dreams are contraband, but they are your only refuge," Jomo's words were a talisman. His voice was melodic and pure in a way I'd never heard him before. He was the Sirens luring a willing Ulysses. Only here, deliverance, not destruction, was the reward.

Even when he removed his hand from under my chin, I continued to keep my face to the sky. A herd of fluffy clouds drifted into view and, for the first time, I was aware of a warm breeze against my skin. It was a different breeze than usually blew in the prison yard; this one carried the scent of seaweed with it. As my eyes followed the clouds, the breeze ebbed and took me as it went. I was stretched on a strip of white sand tucked in a fold between rocky cliffs that slanted down and jutted into the sea like the arms of a lonely lover.

"Free yourself," Jomo coaxed me on. "Your dreams are your only escape."

Saltwater smells filled the air. Waves formed and rolled and foamed and swished and roared onto the beach.

"You can do anything and go anywhere you want."

The same water Magellan had sailed, had drowned Captain Ahab, had floated the Ark, had baptized Jesus now washed my feet.

"You can be anyone you wish to be and there will be no guards to stop you."

The damp bathing suit cooled my skin and the fine sand was gritty under my back as I lay looking at the sky, counting clouds and choosing one to ride out, then back.

"Look," Jomo said, filled with surprise. "Look, there. That cloud. See?" He pointed to a small puff trailing the herd. "That's the same cloud I saw over Kyoto in Japan yesterday."

Now Jomo's cloud was over the flat blonde beach in western Africa where I lay.

"A geisha and I walked in flowers along the Katsura River." Jomo's voice was filled with warm remembrances. "We watched children play and heard doves coo. Later, we sat close and sipped Pearl Dew Tea in the Imperial Villa while the white-faced Kabuki rehearsed."

I lay on a beach towel and marveled at the blend of women around me. They were sunbathing and strolling and swimming; all unashamedly clad in bright-colored wedges of gossamer cloth riding the tight pubic triangle of their dark thighs.

"Then, at sunset," Jomo's voice came from the other side of the world, "we wrote our names with love on that very cloud."

A lone woman gestured. Our eyes met, then smiles came naturally. Her name was the heart of a song. Our hands touched, our minds locked, the earth moved and at that moment, I knew I could walk on water.

"And now," Jomo said, "here comes that cloud again to give me a second chance."

"Yes, Jomo," I said; my voice came trembling from far away. "It comes to give us both a second chance."

From then on, everyday, Jomo and I stood on our spot with our backs against the brick building. Sometimes we would transport each other with whispered visions. At other times we would escape alone, silently watching our visions merge with the sky.

One morning after breakfast, Jomo said as we started across the yard, "They took Spokane last night."

"Spokane Mack?" I asked, not sure what he was talking about.

"Yeah. Took him to the mental hospital," Jomo said. "He lost his grip, couldn't cope any longer and tried to hang-up. The nightwatch cut him down in time."

"Damn shame," I said, then asked, "what happened?"

"He found out that his woman's been shacking with the cop who busted him."

A maintenance gang was busy repairing the facade of a cell

block building. One of the gang glanced at us, shook his head, then mumbled something I couldn't understand, nor did I care to. We stepped around him and went on.

"Suicide is a lonely way to free yourself," Jomo said.

"Never thought that Spokane Mack would crack up."

"When a man outlives his image," Jomo said somewhat philosophically, "and has nothing else, he's bound to crack."

We went on around the basketball court. A game was just getting started. Tankcar came toward us. He looked small, alone and vulnerable without Spokane Mack at his side. His customary swagger was gone; now he moved at a slow shuffle. His head was lowered, his muscles looked flabby and unused and he was mumbling to himself.

Jomo nudged me and whispered, "Word has it that Tankcar's woman is also getting it from a cop."

Tankcar shuffled past. He didn't seem to notice us. His eyes were deep hollows in his face and looked about as sad as a fortune teller's fate.

"The biggest danger in prison is the psychological scarring, not the physical," Jomo said as we arrived at our spot.

Three months after my first escape, Jomo was released. We had shared daydreams and through our visions had become friends. Yet, on the day he was released from prison, we didn't say good-bye. I was standing against the building, flying with an eagle in the sky.

We flew over the Rocky Mountains, then east, then east some more.

I came to earth in ancient Timbuktu. The tart aroma of fresh camel dung prickled my nostrils as I strolled the baked clay streets to the market square in the shadow of the great Dyinuree Mosque. Senagalese, Bantu and Bambute tradesmen bartered candies and nuts and cheese, spice and dried fruit for salt bricks mined from the pits at Taoudenni. From open-front booths, Songhai merchants sold Arab cloth, Moorish jewelry and belly dancers born at the mouth of the Nile, while derelicts asked alms and floral-tailed peacocks strutted nearby.

In the dry noon shade of a palm, I sat on a Persian rug, and my feet cooled in the crystal Oasis of Amen-Ra. There I sipped quick-chilled pomegranate juice laced with anisette served by mulatto eunuchs and watched ebony concubines from south of the Sudan parade to the auctioneer's call. That evening, after dining with a nomad prince, I climbed onto a cloud and looking into the coming night sky, I heard the guard sergeant shout: "Okay, you men. Clear the yard. Get your asses back to your cells."

When I returned to the prison, Jomo had gone.

Now, thirteen years later, I still spend my days standing on my spot in the yard. One day, I'll find a new prisoner to pass my secret on to, but for now, I like taking solo flights, drifting wherever I like and escaping in the sky. It's lonely at times, yes, but the greatest thing about being called insane is that no one bothers asking me to explain.

Of course I hear the whispers of inmates and the guards alike. They all call me a space case and they joke about my clean-shaven head. They've nicknamed me The Looney Tune. But I'm immune to all of that. I don't talk to them and they don't talk to me. And I'm glad they pay-me-no-mind. They have no dreams, no visions, therefore, no escape. Their lives are defined by the prison walls.

I'm free.

■

Long Tongue

Long Tongue, the blues merchant, strolls on stage. His
guitar rides sidesaddle against his hip. The drummer slides
onto the tripod seat behind the drums, adjusts the high-hat
cymbal, and runs a quick, off-beat tattoo on the tom-tom,
then relaxes. The bass player plugs into the amplifier, checks
the settings on the control panel and nods his okay. Three
horn players stand off to one side, clustered, lurking like brilliant sorcerer-wizards waiting to do magic with their musical
instruments.

The auditorium is packed. A thousand inmates face the
stage; all anticipate a few minutes of musical escape. The
tear gas canisters recessed in the ceiling remind us that everything is for real.

The house lights go down and the stage lights come up. Reds and greens and blues slide into pinks and ambers and yellows and play over the six poised musicians.

The Blues Merchant leans forward and mumbles, "Listen. Listen here, you all," into the microphone. "I want to tell you about Fancy Foxy Brown and Mean Lean Green. They is the slickest couple in the east coast scene."

Thump. Thump. The drummer plays. Boom-chicka-chicka-boom. He slams his tubs. The show is on. Toes tap. Hands clap. Fingers pop. The audience vibrates. Long Tongue finds his groove. He leans back. He moans. He shouts. His message is picked up, translated and understood. With his soul he releases us from bondage, puts us in tune with tomorrow, and the memories of the cold steel cells—our iron houses—evaporate.

Off to one side, a blue coated guard nods to the rhythm. On the up-beat his eyes meet the guard sergeant's frown. The message is clear: "You are not supposed to enjoy the blues. You get paid to watch, not be human." The message is instantaneously received. The guard jerks himself still and looks meaner than ever.

Long Tongue, The Blues Merchant, wails on. He gets funky. He gets rough. He gets raunchy. His blues are primeval. He takes everybody, except the guards, on a trip. The guards remain trapped behind the prison's walls while, if only for a short time, we are free.

The blues is our antidote, and Long Tongue, The Blues Merchant, is our doctor.

■

Old Gates

Over the years, Old Gates had lost his teeth. The State replaced them with ever-white porcelain ones. They worked well enough but were not the same as the real thing.

Most of his hair had fallen out and the little he had left had turned grey. The steel walls of the cell had sapped his strength, the poor lighting had weakened his eyesight. The cheap mattress had curved his back and he limped on knees smashed by a guard's club. He hadn't had a visitor in eleven years and his only mail was a monthly religious magazine and an occasional throwaway because someone had forgotten to remove his name from an ancient mailing list.

Old Gates was senior man in the License Plate Shop where we stamped out plates for models of cars he'd never seen. He never asked anyone for anything and when he went to the yard he sat alone. Long ago, Old Gates stopped looking at the sky, envying the birds their freedom. Now all that he saw was their droppings. It blighted the yard and he worried about it falling on him.

One night, sick in his cell, Old Gates asked for a doctor. The guard told him that no doctor was on duty at that hour, that he'd have to hang on until morning. But Old Gates was tired of hanging on. He laid down and never got up.

During the morning headcount, the guard found Old Gates cold and still and never having to worry about bird shit again.

■

Crazy Willie

Crazy Willie talked to fairies and counted blades of grass. He spent time with Moses, Dante, Mohammed and Buddha. Even the presidents of the United States were numbered among his daily friends.

When Willie went to church, he spoke with God. The chaplain thought that was worthy, if not spiritually cool. But when Willie insisted that God had spoken to him, the chaplain reported him to the guard sergeant. The sergeant charged Willie with unauthorized communications and turned him over to the shrink. The shrink fitted Willie with a tight white jacket, filled his veins with chemical peace and booked him into a padded cell.

When Willie came back from the mental hospital we still called him Crazy Willie. But Willie wasn't so crazy as not to know that he could talk with no one, except himself, and even then, never out loud.

■

Notes

How are prisoners supposed to be objective about our plight? It's as much of a folly to ask that of a prisoner as to ask it of a man who has his nuts caught in a slam-locked door. Neither can be objective about the pain. And neither should be asked to be.

■

They told me that I was sent to Attica for "re-programming." When I arrived, shackled and chained and begging to get involved, the KKK, operating under the banner of the guard's union, laid a just-hung Puerto Rican boy on the floor. They said that he had died from "hyperactivity."

58

And the guards made jokes about how the boy's choked-swollen tongue propped open his jaw "like a just-boiled hog." And they even refused to allow a white prisoner to close the Rican's dead eyes.

On Sunday, the reverend, who sang "Mammy" while King led the marches, refused to pray for the dead boy's soul. He claimed the warden feared a riot if the Puerto Rican was dignified with prayer.

And the dead Rican's mother could not understand that reprogramming at Attica, when translated into English, means to cut off your own balls and hand them to The Man. Smile and say, "Thank you, sir, for trusting me with the knife."

■

Most prisoners know the rules which govern them far better than most guards whose job it is to enforce those rules. There is nothing confusing about this. In prison it's a normal situation. Just a simple matter of the oppressed knowing more about the nature of his oppression than does the oppressor.

There is little wonder that when a guard is at a loss for the exact rule he feels has been violated, he often substitutes a handy lie for the truth.

Ignorance dictates. In most cases, prison discipline is more a matter of making up rules to create a crime than matching a crime to the written rule.

■

Everything else might be doubtfully organized but the Adjustment Committee, whose job it is to mete out punishment for rule infractions and misbehavior reports, is never in doubt.

This is the only policing force with a hundred percent conviction record. Somehow, something has to be wrong. No one is ever acquitted. With the Adjustment Committee, a prisoner is never right.

■

Prisons are more than places of exile or quarantine. They are the manifestations of the ideologies of the people who run them. And, as we know, ideology—whether steeped in direct and constant physical abuse, or liberalized with psychological and passive violence—merely determines the nature of the repression it spawns.

It precipitates from above.

The worst part of any repression is that the oppressors control it from a distance. Distance precludes human contact. Wherever human contact is absent, inhumanity is rampant.

It is the henchmen of the oppressor who are left to deal with the oppressed. The henchmen are caught inbetween. In prison it is the lowly guard. He is as much of a victim as are the prisoners. But the prisoner quickly learns that a victim of this nature is the most dangerous victim of all.

■

Old speckled-haired Doc has more than thirty years behind the wall. He was released on parole only to have his freedom interrupted with an arrest for a crime for which he was later acquitted and judged not guilty.

But the parole department forced Doc's return to prison anyway. Guilty or not, the fact that he was arrested is considered a violation of parole. And the law against double jeopardy does not apply.

■

"Hey, brother," Sparrow called Demon to a halt. "I need some info."

"Sure thing," Demon said, always willing to rap, "what'll it be?"

"When a woman wants to give a man some money," Sparrow said awkwardly, somewhat embarrassed, "how do you take it gracefully."

"You mean, how do you get the money," Demon clarified the question, "and not make it seem like you're playing game on her?"

"Yeah. Exactly."

"Well," Demon picked his words like a chicken feeding in a rocky yard, "you just let her know that normally you wouldn't be broke but the prison situation done got you down and doing bad and has forced you to come to her for temporary relief."

Sparrow thought it over, then asked, "Is that it?"

Demon said, "One more thing."

"What?"

"Make sure that she understands to give all that she can get."

Sparrow thought it over again, thanked Demon for the help, then strutted across the prison yard to where Miss Joy, a grey-haired, wrinkled-face homo lounged against the wall.

∎

We laughed and jived and bullshitted all the way to the Mess Hall.

Our guards thought that with the lure of an overcooked rib steak and mashed potatoes our spirits had finally been broken; that we had forgotten what had happened at Attica.

When we got into the Mess Hall, we didn't eat; we didn't talk. Our jive and bullshit had been checked at the door and our laughter transformed into a silent indictment. The guards stood in their dishonest boots and twitched in their skins of guilt while we breathed a common breath and lowered our eyes and remembered our history.

Then we laughed and jived and bullshitted all the way back to our cells.

∎

The last time Pete's wife came to see him, she brought a freshly baked ham. Between the times of her visits, Pete had become a Muslim and pork is now an evil to him.

At least that's what Pete says in the open. Privately he begs Allah to forgive him for bowing to the power of a home cooked ham.

∎

"Man, you've got a game for them all," Slim Sam said to slick talking Mackin' Mo.

Mackin' Mo, puffed with self pride, said, coming on slick out of the side of his mouth, "Now days, I'm looking for a ninety year old woman. One that can't walk. She ain't got to come visit. All she's got to do is sit in her wheelchair and write the checks."

"That's what I call real strong game," Slim Sam praised him.

"The old rugged cross was more humane than I am," Mackin' Mo quipped as he watched two homos pass and wondered how he could exploit their talents.

■

Under normal circumstances, Love and Being In Love are beautiful concepts. But to endure in this environment, it's far better to avoid such snares, no matter how enticing the prize might be.

■

I never learned to speak the English language properly. In the school I went to, I was merely taught to make approximate and appropriate sounds. Still, I never thought that I was deprived.

When I was a kid it was ultra cool not to have any homework, and when I got into The Night Life, I was too busy getting money to worry about it.

Now that I have to use prison stationery to write for a parole job, I find myself playing catch up. Playing catch up is not a nice way to be.

■

Exams are designed for the poor. Rich folks don't take exams. They make them up to keep us confused. They hand out an exam and say, "If you pass this we'll let you move up into the 'clique.'" But most of the questions don't have any answers. It's like asking, "How many hairs are on a square inch of a sheep's skin?"

Hell, the only time I ever saw a sheep's skin was when it was on something I stole.

■

"When I go home at night," the cell block guard said, "I forget about this place. I leave my job on the job." He wiped the sweat from his thick red neck and relit his cigar stub. "If I were to think of you prisoners as human beings, like my wife and kids are, I'd never be able to lock you in a cell. Then where would I be?" He flicked cigar ash on the clean floor, then answered his own question. "I would be on welfare because opening and closing cells and counting heads are the only things I know."

I remembered hearing that a guard's job was the highest paid unskilled job in the state but I couldn't feel sorry for him.

He flicked another chunk of ash, then told me to sweep it up before the duty sergeant reported him for having a dirty cell block floor.

■

"How would you pronounce this name?"

He printed W O T O W I T Z on a sheet of paper.

"You mean you don't know how to pronounce your own name?" I looked at the name and tried to figure it out.

"Yeah," he said, "I know my real name, but this is an alias." He pointed to the name on the paper. "I saw it on a store's sign just before the police busted me. And I've been using it ever since."

"I always wondered where a black dude got such a name."

"Now you know."

"How would you say it?" I asked him.

He shriveled up his face like a prune. "Wot-o-wits," he said, "but that don't make it right. I'd really be embarrassed if someone were to check me on it."

"I know what you mean," I said, still trying to puzzle out the name. "That happened to me once. I was using an alias and the police were about to let me go. Then I opened my fat mouth and mispronounced it. All hell broke loose. I ended up doing two-and-a-half-to-five and I still never learned to say that name.

∎

"Why are you packing all that junk?" I asked Seatrain who was to be released the next day.

He was busy stuffing stacks of prison rulebooks, regulations, directives and bulletins outlining every aspect of a prisoner's expected conduct into a large cardboard box.

"When I get home," Seatrain said, "I'm gonna put this stuff on the walls of my walk-in closet. And anytime I get the urge to do wrong I'm gonna smoke a joint and lock myself into that closet and just sit and look at all this shit. Then, I'm gonna ask myself 'Do you really want to risk going through this again?' " He threw in a handful of laundry tickets, Mess Hall menus, hobby permits, passes and other prison miscellanea, closed the box, tied it shut with a rope. "I figure that after about ten seconds of reliving this place, any wrong doing urges I might have will be gone."

"I can dig it," I said, "that's rehabilitation."

"No, man." Seatrain looked around at the steel walls, the cold water sink, the toilet that seldom worked, the narrow cot and the cell bars. "That's just common sense."

I reminded him that common sense ain't so common.

"Maybe not," he said, "but I sure got it."

He dragged the packed box from his cell and I helped him carry it to the outside gate.

∎

I envy maggots, crabs and body lice. They have more opportunities to make love than I do.

■

"I'm in prison as punishment," Mondongo said, "not *for* punishment. So don't take your hostilities out on me."

■

The Soap Opera

All winter Dobbson sat in the South Yard watching his favorite TV soap opera. On the coldest days, Dobbson was there, bundled like an Eskimo, drinking hot coffee from his half-gallon thermos, clapping his mittened hands and stomping his feet to keep the blood flowing. Even when snow blew in ten-foot drifts against the wall, Dobbson was there.

Many times Dobbson would be the only inmate out in the freezing yard and the shivering guard sergeant would plead for him to go inside. But Dobbson would just shake his head and say, "No good. This is my recreation and I'm going to enjoy myself." As long as Dobbson stayed in the yard, a full guard complement also had to stay out. The guards suffered, but Dobbson didn't. He watched his soap opera and forgot the cold.

When spring came Dobbson was joined by other inmates.
They were often loud and sometimes inconsiderate. They
didn't really care for the soap opera and were only watching
because they had no place else to be. But that didn't bother
Dobbson. He was intent on his soap opera and paid them
little attention. He had spent all winter with his soap opera
and now that it was spring, he was in love and his world didn't
include other inmates.

Dobbson's love wasn't the painful kind that people fall into
and out of as if it were a container. It was a freeing love that
offered a fantastic escape, and left him with a gratifying taste
on his lips.

One sunny afternoon a couple of guys were high-jiving
nearby, and one commented, as he watched the female star
of Dobbson's soap opera strut across the video screen, "Man,"
he said, "that there broad sure is a fine looking bitch."

Dobbson stiffened, but said nothing.

"Bet she can handle a joint like a flat-back whore at a cut-
rate fire sale," the other guy said.

The first agreed. "A bitch like that," he said, "will canni-
balize a swipe with one move."

Dobbson turned, looked at the two with cold eyes, and
said, "You men have got to show folks respect."

"Respect? Who? What?"

"The lady on TV," Dobbson said.

"Man, are you crazy?"

The other said, "That bitch is a thousand miles away and
if she was right here, she wouldn't be worth my respect."

"You had better cool your roles," Dobbson warned.
"Don't over sport your hands."

"I can always play my hand," one of the two wolfed, "and
I know a two-bit bitch when I see one. And that there is one."
He pointed to the soap opera's star.

"She ain't no bitch," Dobbson said. His eyes narrowed to
a squint and he sized up the two men. "She's my woman."

Both guys laughed, but Dobbson didn't crack a smile. He
got up quietly and walked away. This wasn't a laughing matter.

When they saw Dobbson returning, they started to laugh again, but they didn't see the steel pipe that Dobbson carried low against his right hip. When they did see it, it was too late to run, or even defend themselves. Dobbson struck. Blood, scalp and hair flew. Two bodies caved to the ground.

"Those guys have got to learn to respect another man's woman," Dobbson said as the guards rushed him away. "They have got to learn respect."

■

Notes

I wake nights. Yesterdays flood my mind. Crowding memories of birds and blue skies and ocean-washed beaches.

Flowers out for Sunday sale and morning news and coffee-flavored love. And crimson sunset watching. Wood paths. New moons and your fingers, finger-drawing daisies and long-stemmed roses on my back.

Dragonfly wings and gossamer and butterflies playing tag—touch and go—controls my nights and leaves me to wonder as sleep crawls back into my head, were you ever real, or nothing more than a jest of my fantasy factory?

Sometimes in the dark, I doubt my own reality.

■

I came across some real poetry last night. Stumbled and got a brain sprain.

"Worse thing about a brain sprain," the doctor said, "is that you can't put a splint on it. Or even an Ace Bandage."

Shit!

"You can ease the pain of a cut jugular vein. But for a brain sprain, where do you fit the tourniquet?"

■

Narcoticized. We lounged against storefront walls.

Hearing empty baby cry hungry and our stomachs gurgle growl and tenement rat scurry—and even gangster cockroaches seemed natural to us.

Until one day.

The storeowner's color TV showed green trees and food and luxuries as real, not myths, and that the pain of living from welfare check to welfare check is not a universal fact.

We smashed the store's window.

Via the pawnshop, we converted the TV into babyfood, three meals a day, rat traps, clothes and rent. In the process we transformed ourselves from a poverty statistic into a self-help program.

■

All the wrong people people my dreams. Like whores on stroll I watch for a friendly sign. The only warmth remembered is my mother's jelly brown breast.

■

They took Silky away.

Overnight, Silky claimed he had a revelation. Said he saw a vision pasted to the wall of his cell. A nude woman with azure eyes, walking on water, stopping only here and there to improvise a few steps of boogie woogie.

When the guards unlocked his cell, Silky stumbled out. He was draped in a blanket; his mug was painted magic marker colors and he proclaimed himself a Seminole Indian Chief, the last direct descendant of that warrior race.

Of course the guards did not believe a word he said. They never did before. Still, they took him seriously enough not to take any chances.

Silky was rushed to the psych's "space station" and logged into a quiet blue room.

The psych judged Silky to be "non-crazy"—at least not any more crazy than is normal in prison. He read the guard's report, frowned and determined that Silky had not broken any rules. Still, the psych—not one to take a chance—prescribed daily Thorazine, a multitude of muscle relaxants and ordered an around-the-clock watch on Silky's actions.

In prison, not even the psychiatrist will make allowances for a prisoner changing his history, making his kind of escape.
■

Skeeter Mack

Skeeter Mack, who had survived head on collisions and self-inflicted madness, switchblades and poison, hair dyes and niggers—both black and white, rattlesnake bites, flat-back hookers, Mad Dog wine and sudden wealth, refused to accept as fact that his only options were to become an expert at gin rummy and a grandmaster at mail order chess.

In the old days, when Skeeter Mack walked the prison yard, even the redneck guards called him Mr. Nigger. This was at a time when everyone else was just plain, ordinary, everyday nigger. Skeeter Mack deserved that kind of respect.

As times changed the nature of crimes and the kinds of criminals changed, Skeeter Mack withdrew from the bustle of the Main Yard into a tight corner of older cronies who stationed themselves in the smaller side yard.

Skeeter Mack said that his withdrawal was a shield to guard against the poetic glibness of the new breed prisoner who buffed their shit like dance hall wax and polished their acts like redundant whores on stroll.

One spring day following the equinox, while brushing off a hustle—a game played on his spirit—Skeeter Mack reached out and damaged the eyes, lips and rib cage of the popcorn pimp who confronted him.

Skeeter Mack was instantaneously reclassified and listed as a "free-lance lunatic." Six months later he was paroled after being processed through a psychiatric door. He was certified cured but lame-brained.

Convinced by the system that poachers make the best game wardens, Skeeter Mack took a nightwatchman's job. He oversaw a fancy graveyard and other active stables of nouveau rich liberals who prided themselves on hiring an ex-con.

He arranged his sleeping hours so that he would have ample time each day to patrol the parking lot directly across from the prison gate. He watched the gate—alone, bedraggled, cronyless—like a spent horse homesick for the stable. A beached sailor watching the sea.

Each day at shift change time, Skeeter Mack would exchange greetings and assorted niceties with the guards and other workers coming to and leaving the prison. He even had a kind word for the warden. The only person he would not speak to, wave to or share a nod with, was the psychiatrist. He blamed the psychiatrist for disrupting his prison life by suggesting parole and forcing freedom on him.

While on station in the parking lot, Skeeter Mack would relive his prison born memories. The memories were as elaborate as those of the Ringling Brothers and Salvador Dali. He remembered every prison face, every prison joke and the hard times too. He was alone, but his memories of prison kept him company.

One day, two wise ass jitterbugs approached him. They were fooled by their anger and leaped at Skeeter Mack. The youngsters mistook him for a weak old man but Skeeter Mack, who often said, "I ain't get this far in life by being no victim," refused to allow them to beat notes on his skull.

When the ambulance arrived at the nearest hospital, the two angry jitterbugs were tagged and slid into an icebox to await their next of kin.

Skeeter Mack refused to plead self-defense, even refused to give details of the attack so that court appointed attorneys could help him. Instead he copped out to the DA's offer and left the courtroom in chains.

Once again Skeeter Mack sits in the tight corner of older cronies. Now he happily shares the memories of his night-watchman days, the memory of a real steak dinner and the yield of a woman's soft flanks. His cronies glue their minds to his every word—a ledge to view the outside world, a link between the past and the future. Skeeter Mack has been where every prisoner dreams of going.

Still, when the work shifts change, Skeeter Mack stands near the entrance gate—this time, inside looking out. He smiles as he welcomes the guards and others to another day's work. He even welcomes the warden to what he calls "Skeeter Mack's prison." The warden, of course, chuckles in an understanding way and thanks Skeeter Mack for the welcome.

Although he is now deemed "clinically safe" and reclassified a "resident lunatic," the psychiatrist is still the only one Skeeter Mack will not speak to. He turns his back whenever the psychiatrist comes to work. But in the tight corner, in the smaller yard, Skeeter Mack confides in his oldest cronies that his greatest fear is the psychiatrist will force freedom on him again.

■

Notes

I guzzled a batch of jailhouse booze. Then I did two sets of
pushups—fifty pushups each set—weightlifted two hundred
pounds ten times and called a fellow prisoner a lively bunch of
multi-motherfuckers.

He laughed me off, gave the "Peace" and "Power" salutes
followed by a shout of "Right on, my brother man." Then he
strolled away, along the yard, shaking his head as he went. He
understood my condition. I was burning off prison tension.
Nothing personal. He knew everything in a flash because the
day before he used me in the same way I used him.

"What goes 'round, comes 'round," I thought as I waved
the salutes at his back and relaxed against the wall.

I was cool!

■

"You would do better picking your victims with more care," the doctor suggested as he stitched the gash in Lame Jones' head. "This is the third time in two months that your plots have backfired and sent you to the hospital."

"Yes, sir." Lame grimaced against the pain in his head. "I'll change my approach."

"Good idea." The doctor tied off the last stitch, swabbed away a trickle of oozing blood and taped on a bandage. "I can't keep reporting that you injured yourself falling out of bed."

"Yes, sir," Lame Jones agreed, "Somebody might get suspicious."

"Either that," the doctor said, "or you're going to get yourself killed."

■

The shrink's first question is: "Are you sure that you want to be 'sane'?"

I give it some thought, bounce the thought off the prison wall, weigh the possibilities and answer, "No."

The shrink smiles like a glutton feasting on gourmet cuisine. He stamps my file "UNADJUSTED" and adds my name to the "pay-him-no-mind" list.

The guards hold their clubs at the ready and fellow prisoners whisper behind my back. Everyone stands aside. Even certified-bona fide killers lower their eyes when I pass.

■

Cryin' Shame

Cryin' Shame was the ugliest of the ugly homos who pranced the prison yard. Razor scars from gut bucket barroom fights lined his potmarked face like strings on a gypsy's guitar, and when he grinned his snaggle-tooth mouth issued a breath as funky as ten day old mustard greens on a hot summer night. Cryin' Shame was so ugly, it was rumored, that when the judge sentenced him to life in prison he was given an extra year for violating the Environmental Protection Act.

No one ever voluntarily gave Cryin' Shame any action. Not even those asshole bandits who had been in prison, and womanless for eons and were known to fuck anything hot and hollow had the heart to pick Cryin' Shame. The asshole bandits would opt in favor of their memories or fantasies of pre-prison sexual exploits and a greased fist rather than confront the horror of Cryin' Shame's mug.

Over the years, seeded with sexual deprivation, Cryin' Shame had developed a quick, one punch knockout blow. When the mood hit and his female side longed to be satisfied, Cryin' Shame would engage his prey in pleasant, small talk conversation and coax him off to a quiet, little traveled spot. Then, with his one punch, Cryin' Shame would stun his victim and take what he wanted. As a result, very few unarmed people ever talked to Cryin' Shame. Even the guards kept their distance.

Each time the courts sentenced a new shipment of pigmeat to the prison, Cryin' Shame would be loitering near the reception gate, lurking like a misshapen welcome mat.

One hot summer morning when the yard was in full swing with volleyball and basketball, baseball and hand ball, chess, checkers and cards, joggers, weightlifters and popcorn pimps polishing their shit, and no one was left inside, Cryin' Shame stalked a new, innocent looking young dude into the storehouse basement.

Before Cryin' Shame could cock his arm to fire his one punch, or even knew what had hit him, Cryin' Shame's pants had been stripped down around his crusty knees, the cheeks of his bottomless ass had been spread and lightly greased, and the young, innocent looking dude's cum was trickling from Cryin' Shame's butt.

That afternoon, smiling and sashaying like a love-struck school girl, Cryin' Shame displayed the bruises mashed on his chin by the young dude's fist and boasted how he had been raped with tender, loving care.

For days afterward Cryin' Shame hung out in the storehouse basement. He waited like a mark to be mugged. After a week had passed and nothing happened—not even an accidental bump followed by an apologetic "Excuse me "—Cryin' Shame shuffled around the exercise yard and lamented that a one punch love affair is worse than no love affair at all.

■

Notes

"Yo, man," Peat Moss called out from the cell next to mine. "Anybody got any of that scientific milk?"

"Huh?" Eighty odd voices shouted back. "What the fuck is 'scientific milk'?"

The few who didn't shout, laughed.

"You know, that powdered stuff," Peat Moss shouted again, "that shit what you put in coffee."

Everyone fell quiet as if trying to figure a riddle.

I found the answer. "Coffee creamer," I called back to Peat Moss. "Synthetic milk?" I asked, "is that what you want?"

"Yeah, that's it." Peat Moss didn't miss a beat. "That's what I said. Scientific milk!"

"Scientific milk." I kept my mouth shut and thought as I passed the creamer through my cell bar and next door to Peat Moss. "My God, what a dastardly cor-rip-shen of the languish."

■

"Sure," the old line guard spit a gob of tobacco juice into a tin cup as he explained to the new recruit fresh on the job from the training academy. "I know which prisoners are making wine. I know which are fucking the fags. I know which are smoking dope and breaking all the other rules too. I know everything everybody is doing. That's my job." He gave a smug smile, then spat another gob of tobacco juice into the cup. "But so what?" he said. "Ain't nobody killing nobody and ain't nobody trying to escape."

The old line guard read the confusion on the recruit's face, patted him on the back and proclaimed, "As long as they're happy not trying to get out, I'm happy letting them break the rules."

The young guard was staggered. His mouth hung open like the rear flap on a dump truck. He was hearing everything the academy had trained him against.

"Look at it this way." The old timer offered the recruit a plug of tobacco. "Just remember, you can't stop everything and run a good prison too."

After a few more on the job training sessions the new recruit learned to get along by going along, to pass the buck and cover his ass. He also learned to chew tobacco, shoot the juice with amazing accuracy, look the other way and to get a slice of the pie in the process.

■

Cleanhead Meets Dale Carnegie

I was coming down the long stairway from the tailor's shop above the prison's bathhouse when I met September Red and Fast Eddie The Gypper coming up. They were carrying bundles of inmate uniforms to be repaired and reissued. This was their once a day assignment, and they went about it with the same haphazard air as any other inmate would—just a way of passing the time.

"Hey, now, Jay," Red said. He held out his right hand, palm up.

"What is it?" I slapped his hand in greeting.

"Same old, same old."

"Nothing changed but the address," Fast Eddie said. "Everything's for real."

I knew the feeling and said so.

"Johnson's back," Red said as he lowered his bundle to the stairs.

"Which Johnson?"

"Cleanhead," Fast Eddie answered. He hiked his bundle higher, more comfortable on his back.

"No shit," I said. "When did he show?"

"This morning. Two marshals brought him back," Red said, then asked for a cigarette.

I shook one free from the pack. He dropped it into his shirt pocket and said he'd smoke it later.

"Was it a parole violation?"

"Naw," Fast Eddie said, "the dude's got a brand new beef."

"Shit."

"Two-and-a-half-to-five."

"And he still owed a deuce on the old sentence," Red added.

"What's the bust for this trip?"

"Same old stuff," Fast Eddie said. "Snatching other folk's stuff in the middle of the night."

"Burglary?"

"That's what the law calls it."

"Had to be," Fast Eddie said. "Cleanhead didn't live there and he sure as hell didn't have no key."

"Damn shame," I said. "Cleanhead just left here three months ago."

"He's back now," Red said.

A guard coming up the stairs squeezed past us. He went a few steps higher, then turned and, in a shaky but gruff tone, told us to move on.

"Don't panic," Red mumbled. "We ain't plotting."

"What was that?" The guard stepped up another step, putting a little more space between us, but his voice was harsher. "You some kind of smart ass?"

"No," Red stared up at him. "We're just taking these things to the tailor's shop."

"Then get on with it," the guard snarled as he backed up a few more steps, then turned and climbed on toward the top.

Red chuckled and lifted his bundle onto his shoulder.

"Some dudes feel better in prison than out," Fast Eddie said as he and Red started up the stairs again.

"Don't think that's Cleanhead's problem." I flatten against the wall so they could pass.

"What is?" Red asked.

"He just don't know how not to get busted."

Fast Eddie laughed. "That's his problem, yours and mine, Red's and everybody's in the joint."

"That's the real deal," I said, then, looking up at them, asked, "Where is he?"

"C Block. Reception Company," Red shouted back as they went up.

I pushed open C Block's door and looked around for the guard. He wasn't in sight.

"Cleanhead's back," Big Shorty, the Reception Company's clerk said as I stepped inside.

"I got the wire," I said. "What cell is he in?"

"Eight twenty-five. But you can't see him."

"No?"

"He'll be locked in 'til the Security Office ok's him for the yard."

"When will that be?"

"Tomorrow sometime."

"Can I run down and yell at him?"

"Not with McGraw on duty," Big Shorty lowered his voice. "That redneck would put us both in segregation."

We agreed that McGraw was a mother fucker.

"Tight. By the book," Big Shorty said. "He sees evil in everything."

We heard keys jingling, knew that McGraw had finished his rounds and was headed back to the reception desk.

"When you get a chance," I said quickly, "give Cleanhead my hello."

"Sure thing."

"If he needs anything, let me know."

Big Shorty nodded.

I stepped through the door, out into the bright sun, and went across the Main Yard to the Gym for my afternoon workout.

It was two days later and raining when I ran into Cleanhead. He had just come from the Barber Shop where he had had his head freshly shaved, his scalp shampooed, massaged and oiled.

"Damn sorry to see you back."

"That's two of us," Cleanhead said.

The rain formed into beads on his slippery head, then slid down onto his jacket collar.

"What went down?" I asked.

"Got caught behind enemy lines without proper ID," he joked.

We walked through the Control Gate, showed our passes to the guard, then started across the yard toward the Library.

"Seriously."

"Can't figure it out," Cleanhead said.

We flashed Peace and Power signs at two other inmates going in the opposite direction. They returned the greeting.

"Did a good job," he said. "Didn't break a glass. Didn't make a sound. Didn't leave a fingerprint."

"A clean job is your trademark," I said.

Big Shorty hurried toward us. He was all hassled and blown out of shape, splashing through the puddles and struggling to keep his balance, a goat jumping rope backwards.

"What you doing out in the rain?" I shouted at Big Shorty.

"That fucking McGraw is sending me for supplies."

"Somebody's got to do it," I said as he neared.

"Ain't my job," Big Shorty wiped the rain from his forehead. "McGraw is being a prick."

"He's a hack," Cleanhead said. "That's his role."

"Just hold your peace," I said to Big Shorty as he came abreast and passed us. "Everything will be cool."

"Shit," Big Shorty snorted.

He waved his pass at the guard and splashed on through the Control Gate.

At the Library we shook the rain from our jackets and went in. A few guys were reading newspapers and magazines, others were wearing headphones and snapping their fingers to the music and mouthing the lyrics as they listened, but most were just keeping out of the rain. We took two books from the shelf and sat at a side table with them open in front of us.

I asked Cleanhead again how the bust went down.

"That," he emphasized the word, "I still can't figure. Everything was smooth, like polished glass."

"Maybe a sick junkie ratted you out for a fix?"

We kept our voices low, giving the guard no reason to hassle us.

"Naw," he said. "Nobody knew about the job but me."

"And of course the police and the victim."

"That was after the fact," he said. "I just can't figure how they knew it was me." He fluttered the pages of the book with his thumb, then let it lay open at a random page. "It was a clean job." There was the edge of pride in his voice. "It was polished. Brilliant. I was Rembrandt creating a masterpiece." He fluttered the pages again, then shut the book and pushed it from him. "I left no traces," he said. "I only took things I knew I could get rid of quickly. I checked and rechecked everything. Still, three days later, the police showed at my place and busted me."

"Think carefully," I said. "Something's got to fit. The police ain't psychic. They don't use a Ouija board."

He shook his head and shrugged and said, "Hell, Jay, I did it the same as I always do a job."

We leaned back in the chairs and were quiet for a long while. Then I said, "That's your answer?"

"What's my answer?"

"Your super-clean, smooth, professional M.O."

"My what?"

"Your *modus operandi*. That's Latin," I said.

"I know it's Latin. Now run it to me in English."

"Your mode of operation." I broke it down for him. "Your method of doing a job."

His defenses shot up. "I always do a professional job."
There was an irate edge to his voice. "I'm never sloppy, and
I do all burglaries the same way."

"And that's what got you busted."

"Being professional?"

"No," I said. "Not being professional enough got you
busted."

"Bullshit," Cleanhead said. "I'm a pro. A real pro."

"Ain't no pros in prison."

"Fuck you, Jay," he said and stood up.

"Sit down. Relax and listen."

He sat down slowly but stayed tense and on the edge of
the chair.

"A real pro," I said, "never does the same thing twice. He
always changes his routine. Invents new ways," I told him.
If I had learned nothing else in prison, I learned that. "You
didn't, and now you're back in the joint."

He stared at me. Cold. Then his defensive shield left him,
he slid back in the chair and was ready to talk again.

"What else could it be?" I leaned closer to him. "No wit-
nesses. No rats. And the stuff you took couldn't be traced.
Right?"

He nodded and said slowly, "So the only thing they had to
go on was the way I did the job."

"Right."

"And that's what got me busted, huh?"

"All they had to do was check the files and fit the method
and the burglar together."

"And I fit."

"Must," I said, "and you being back here is proof enough."

"Damn," he said and leaned far back in the chair.

Three weeks later, Cleanhead was assigned to the school's
office as a clerk. He couldn't type, couldn't file and knew
nothing about keeping records. But he was jailwise and knew
how to tell the Job Assignment Committee what they wanted
to hear.

86

"Hey, Jay," Cleanhead called me to a halt as I was coming from the Mess Hall.

I stepped toward him. "How's the job?" I asked.

"It's an all day gig, but it beats slaving in the License Plate Shop."

"True."

We stepped aside to make way for the guys returning a load of empty food trays to the Mess Hall from the Segregation Housing Unit.

"Best thing," Cleanhead said, "I get a lot of free time to do my own thing."

"That's hip. A dude's personal program is far more important than the official one they set up."

The loudspeakers sounded: "Return to the shops, school and the cell blocks. The yard is closed." A guard moving casually, but with a mission, told a small group to move on. Another guard came in our direction.

"Which way you headed?" I asked Cleanhead.

"School," he said. "Back to work."

"I'll give you a walk over."

We moved off just as the guard opened his mouth to speak.

"I'm re-digging my role," Cleanhead said as we walked toward the school yard gate. "Checking out new angles and pulling loose ends together."

"Prison is the time for re-grouping."

"That M.O. thing could have me coming back to prison for the rest of my life." We waved to September Red and Fast Eddie The Gypper. They were struggling with their bundles, going toward the tailor's shop. "And the worst part," Cleanhead said, "I wouldn't even know why."

"Most guys ain't hip to it. Some never will be."

"Glad you turned me on," he said. "I thought I was a pro, and wasn't nothing but popcorn."

We went through the gate and were counted in by the guard and crossed the school yard and went inside.

"I got a lot of rebuilding to do," Cleanhead said as he eased into his chair.

"We all got that to do." I sat on the edge of the desk. "There ain't no success stories in prison."

"This is one that's going to be a success." He pulled open a desk drawer and handed me a full-page Dale Carnegie ad torn from a magazine. The line: "Learn to utilize your abilities more effectively" was underlined and circled in red. "You hip to this dude?" he asked.

"Yeah, I know about D.C.," I joked. "It's a course for white collar con players." Then asked, "You planning to get into it?"

"Already ordered the book." He dropped the ad back into the drawer and slid it shut. "When I hit the streets this time, my shit is really going to be on high point."

Three guys came into the office and asked about changes in class schedules. Cleanhead referred them to the clerk across the room.

"No more picking locks, and climbing in other folk's windows." He leaned back with his hands cupped behind his head. "I'm changing my game completely," he said. "I'll be dipping into a new trick bag for each job I do. With this D.C. jive under my belt, I'll be coming off so slick at the mouth the victims will thank me for choosing them."

An educational counselor leaned through the door and asked Cleanhead to locate a student.

"I'll see that you get him," he said to the counselor.

Cleanhead opened a card file and fingered through it until he came to the student's card, then rechecked the name and prison number to make sure it was the right person.

"Come on." Cleanhead got up. "Walk me to get this guy from class."

In the hall a guard was hassling a student for not having a pass. The guard was puffed up and loud, but the student held his peace and turned and went off to get a pass. The guard looked at us but said nothing. We stepped around him and went on.

Cleanhead said, "I'm rehabilitation in action."

I laughed at the unlikely combination of Cleanhead and Dale Carnegie and said, "That's a big switch. Cat burglar to con man."

"It's still burglary," he said. "Only now I'll be climbing into folks' heads to get them to give what I want instead of climbing through their windows and taking it."

"A lot safer too," I added.

He opened the classroom door, stepped inside and gave the teacher the student's name and number, then came out.

"Hell," he said as we walked back toward the office, "I'll always be a burglar."

"No doubt about that," I said.

Big Shorty turned into the hall, waved and came to us.

"Word on the drum has it," Big Shorty said, "that Slick Roland got busted in The City again for purse snatching."

"That dude's beyond repair," I said. "He should be hospitalized, not penalized."

"He just needs some D.C.," Cleanhead said.

"What's that?" Big Shorty asked.

"A burglar's disguise," Cleanhead said. We both kept a straight face and left Big Shorty flatfooted in the hallway.

We passed the guard and the student again. This time the student had a pass. He showed it to the guard, then went grinning along the hall.

"By using D.C.," Cleanhead said as we returned to the office, "the M.O. will never be the same."

"How do you figure?"

He sat in the chair and jacked his feet onto the desk.

"The only M.O. will be in the method the victim gives it up, not in how I take it." He was enjoying the logic and took his time breaking it down for me. "No two victims will ever give it up the same way," he said. "The M.O. will be different every time."

"Seems to me," I said, "you done found the real deal."

He opened the drawer and said, "You want to see that ad again?"

I thought about it for a moment. "Why not?" I asked. "Everybody here needs a little rehabilitation."

He handed me the ad and said, "Keep it. Pass it on to the next guy."

■

Juanito

And the guards storm the yard sixty strong. They come four abreast. Shoulder to shoulder. Sweat drips from their rednecks like spit from a jackel's jaw. They refuse a one-to-one, man-to-man fight. They are heroes in a mob.

Their tear gas rolls on us like fog covering a seafront. We retreat, coughing and gagging on our vomit, against the prison wall. And cover our heads with folded arms to protect them against their clubs and pickax handles. Even those prisoners not involved are dragged by their heels and beaten until their blood refuses to flow.

Only quiet little Juanito stands his ground. He shouts, a breeze against the hurricane. "Better it is to die in laughter than in tears to live."

Nine months later we are released from The Hole. The bread and water, oatmeal and salted coffee we were fed twice a day is behind us. Now our stomachs will not hold down solid food. Our eyes are weak and burn in the light. After The Hole, our legs ache from lack of exercise.

It is then we hear how the jackals pulled Juanito from his cell, stripped him naked and dragged him to torture him in private, crowding around like buzzards drawn to carrion.

And we hear how the head jackal put his nightstick across Juanito's throat and the point of his knee against Juanito's spine. And how the head jackal yanked until Juanito's neck snapped like a fragile crystal wand caught in a vise.

And the other jackals—caricatures of men—cheered and stamped their jackboots onto quiet little Juanito's twisted body. And called Juanito "Spic" and stamped until Juanito's ribs caved in. The boots that kicked after that only moved the broken parts around.

And we hear how the head jackal drove twenty-five miles to find a doctor who signs the death certificate and swears that Juanito hanged himself. The prison doctor, sober for once, refused to be a part of that lie.

And we hear how Juanito, enduring his ground, laughed. And his laugh made proud the ghost of his forefathers who rode to the end with Zapata and laughed to the end with Zapata and passed that laugh—the song of life—on to Juanito.

And we ask our forefathers to forgive us as we hear Juanito's voice crowned with yesterday's blood calling across time into this dead place, urging us to laugh in the jackal's face, not live with tears in our hearts.

And while we know that Juanito was right to die laughing, our fears conjure us to stand in our cells and have our heads counted like unfilled bottles on a Coca-Cola production line.

■

Habeas Corpus

"Hey, Carlos," Slow Joe called along the row of cells, "How do you spell 'Habeas Corpus'?"

Since Slow Joe was struggling with an appeal of the criminal conviction which brought him to prison, Carlos gladly spelled Habeas Corpus for him.

"Hey, Carlos," Slow Joe called again, this time interrupting Carlos' bedtime reading, "How do you spell 'Circumstantial Evidence'?"

Carlos laid the smut magazine aside, tested his voice to be sure that no traces of being annoyed showed through. Then he spelled 'Circumstantial Evidence.'

Slow Joe thanked him.

After a while, Carlos tucked himself into bed and turned out his light and went upstairs with a big breasted woman fantasized from the centerfold of the magazine.

The woman strutted nude, explicit and in living color through the twilight of Carlos' sleep. There was no need for 'hellos' or other time-wasting, getting-to-know-you foreplay. Carlos vented the shutters of his imagination and had just slipped into the woman and bucked twice when Slow Joe called again.

Carlos pushed himself up and reached for the woman. The steel walls and a brace of cell bars greeted his hand.

"Hey, Carlos," Slow Joe shouted, "How do you spell 'Victim of Circumstances'?"

Carlos shook the newly arriving sleep from his head, silently cursed Slow Joe for interrupting his dream and answered, "It's spelled M-E."

Slow Joe was quiet for a long time, then he shouted back. "Hey, Carlos, are you sure it's M-E? That don't sound right."

■

Notes

The secrets of American justice are learned in dark places, like a prison cell.

Authorities issue a book of rules—"Standards of Inmate Behavior"—the Constitution of Attica. But it is only when you confront the authorities, ask them to live by their own rules, do you learn the unwritten rules—the law behind the law. And even then it is given with a grudge.

Authorities volunteer nothing.

■

When the chief psychiatrist fired his inmate clerk, the guard sergeant asked, "Why?"

"He's a model prisoner, the kind the system is proud to produce." The shrink described the clerk to the sergeant, then went on to explain. "But he has been on the job for two full years and two years is long enough for any person to work any job."

The sergeant raised an eyebrow but wisely kept his mouth shut. The psychiatrist, like J. Edgar Hoover, knows something about everybody. Not even the warden will speak against him.

After the prisoner was recycled and readjusted from clerk with responsibility to a clean-up man with mop and broom, the sergeant asked the psychiatrist, jokingly, of course, if the shrink planned to change jobs also. "Maybe," the sergeant chuckled, "you will reassign yourself from the head of the 'Space Station' to a mess hall cook."

Of course, in public, the psych laughed it off. But in private he made a note in the guard sergeant's file.

Now every time a new batch of replacements arrive from the training academy, the sergeant looks over his shoulder, like the mark in a loaded crap game as he waits for the ax to fall.

■

It is a poor spider that builds its web in the corner of my cell.

■

When they let George out of his cell, he walked straight to the middle of the Main Yard and sat down.

"Fuck it," George said, crossing his legs and making himself comfortable. "Fuck this prison and fuck everything else. The judge sentenced me to do time and this is how I'm going to do it." He spat out a few curse words, then tacked on, "My way."

When the tear gas cleared, George was little more than a pile of flesh dripping blood. Four guards dragged him from the yard and into the mental hospital.

"Fuck it all," George said through the broken teeth, smashed by a guard's club. "If they think I'm crazy now, just wait until I really start doing my time."

■

I look into the mirror: there is no reflection. My days are empty. No friends to ask my whereabouts. Not even an enemy to curse me.

■

Carl's wife sent him a "Dear John." He threw the letter into the toilet and the toilet threw it back.

■

I used to have a large, nude pin-up on my wall. It was there, across from the bed, doing time just as I am. Until I woke from a wet dream and in the half light I thought I had a midget in the cell with me.

When fantasies become that real it's time to give them up.

The next time I pin up a photograph it will be of something I can use—like a helicopter.

■

A sure sign that a prison is mismanaged shows when the homos grow beards, lift weights and talk with deep, bass voices.

When that happens, the warden had better get his shit together or start looking for a new job.

■

The warden got on the in-prison radio and spoke to the prison population. He explained the limitation on the little we are allowed, promised nothing and sold threats with the polish of an unlicensed street vendor. Then, in closing, to show what a nice guy he really is, he wished us all a Merry Christmas.

■

Shing-a-Ling, China and the Note

Once upon a time in the joint, there was Shing-a-Ling.

As prison slick kids go, Shing-a-Ling was a minor leaguer, but you could never tell him that.

We both worked in the prison's maintenance shop. He was in charge of tools: he'd issue them, receive them, clean and put them away. I handled the inventories, the typing and the filing. There was never much work and plenty of time to talk.

One summer's day, while working and listening to Aretha Franklin sing, "You Send Me" over the shop's radio, Shing-a-Ling said to me: "LeRoy, I'm in love. In love like a mudder-fucker."

"Beautiful," I said. "Solid on that. Who's the lucky broad?" as I went on with my work.

"The new homo."

"The new what?" I put my work aside and looked at him.

"The new homo. Name is China 'cause of that mellow, high yellow shine, and them chinky eyes."

"Wait one minute," I said. "Give me a replay. Slow-drag that past again."

"She digs me."

"She? That's a man," I emphasized the words. "A man. Spelled M-A-N. Man."

"I know." He lit a cigarette and blew a cloud of smoke. "But the dude is fine. Super fine."

"You crazy?"

"No jive."

"Shit."

"No bull. I'm serious." He pushed himself up from the chair and bopped around the room. "I laid my heaviest game down, and LeRoy, China went for it. Fact is, the homo ain't have no choice 'cept to go for it. Couldn't resist." He laughed and slapped his thighs. "Man, when Shing-a-Ling plays the tune, everybody dances."

"You better cool your role." I sipped my coffee and went back to filing the morning maintenance reports. "Next," I said, "you'll be strutting and swishing and carrying on around here like a go-go dancer."

"I'm a thoroughbred player." He poured himself a cup of my coffee, mixed in cream and sugar, took a sip and said, "I'm a pimp, not a simp. I can con a swan. My game is playing game, not being a lame."

"Don't pad your part," I cautioned him, "If you'll deal, you'll shuffle. So, dig yourself."

Another routine week of prison life passed. The matter was out of mind until Shing-a-Ling said, "Dig it, LeRoy. I got that broad uptight. The chick really digs me."

"Who?" I was busy typing the monthly inventory.

"China. The homo. Remember?"

I continued to hunt and peck on the typewriter and asked, "What makes you figure 'it' digs you?"

"Keep this under your hat, LeRoy." He grinned and his face radiated pride. "Read this bulletin the broad laid on me."

Shing-a-Ling handed me the note which I unfolded with caution. It was a plainly printed message and I almost died choking back my laughter.

"Hey good buddy," I smiled up at him. "Are you sure this is the right note?"

"Damn is."

"Then, what makes you think that your game is on target?"

"Says so right there." He pointed to the note in my hand. "Says she loves me."

"Man," I asked as discreetly as possible, "can you read?"

The smile drained from his face.

"What do it say, LeRoy?" His voice went a whisper.

"Here." I held the note out to him. "Read it again."

Shing-a-Ling hesitated. "LeRoy," he said, "I can't read."

"Man, spare me the dumb shit."

"Really, I can't."

"Don't pull that I-can't-read game on me." I laughed.

He stood fallen-shouldered and looking at the floor.

"LeRoy." His voice was humble. "Not more than three people in this here joint know the truth, but man, I really can't read."

The humor was gone.

I looked up at him, and looked at the note, and remembered the many times I had watched Shing-a-Ling lug his tomb of sport facts and records through the Control Gate and into the maintenance shop—coming like Moses down the mountain to settle an angry argument. How many times had I laughed as he defiantly hurled the volumes down and spat out the challenge: "There, you jive turkey. Read page 634. Read and weep." He'd shout, "Read out loud, so everybody can hear how dumb you really are."

And too, how many times had I played the sucker and lunged for the greasy pig by going for his letter-from-home game—always starting with him moping around in a blue mood and ending with me being hustled into reading his mail aloud.

And in the Main Yard, when dealing with the smut merchants, Shing-a-Ling would say, "Dig it. I read slow, so just mark off the pages where the action is heavy; where they is gettin' down to the real funky stuff. Mark the pages and I'll take it from there." Then later that evening in the cell block, after we were all locked in and settled for the night, Shing-a-Ling would break the quiet with loud guffaws and bumps against his neighbor's wall until one of them would holler over to him, "Hey man, what the fuck is with you?" And Shing-a-Ling would reply, "Homeboy, this book is a mudderfucker. These people is gettin' down to some real freaky mess." That was the lure. As soon as the guy would say "Turn me on to it," Shing-a-Ling would know that he had him hooked. And after a little more baiting and high-jiving—just enough to tighten the knot—Shing-a-Ling would say, "All right. Here." He'd pass the book through the bar and over to the next cell. "Read those pages where it's marked," Shing-a-Ling would say. "Read it out loud. Read it so that I can hear, too."

And that's the way it always went.

Now he was standing in front of me saying, "Please read the note. LeRoy, what do China say?"

I was embarrassed for him. Still, he insisted I read the note.

"YOU JIVE-TIME SONOFABITCH," I read China's message aloud. "YOU AIN'T MAN ENOUGH FOR ME. FURTHERMORE, THAT THING BETWEEN YOUR LEGS THAT YOU CALL A COCK AIN'T NOTHING BUT A HANDLE FOR ME TO TURN YOU OVER WITH. SO, IF YOU EVER TRY YOUR POPCORN-PIMP SHIT WITH ME, YOU WILL SOON FIND OUT WHO THE REAL WHORE IS." The note was signed, "CHINA," with a postscript: "DON'T FUCK WITH ANYTHING THAT YOU CAN'T HANDLE."

When I had finished reading, Shing-a-Ling was devastated. He said nothing. He just took the note from my hand and folded it into his shirt pocket and walked from the shop.

He didn't return to work that day. And when he didn't show up the next morning, I went looking for him.

On my way across the yard I ran into Niffty Green, one of Shing-a-Ling's slick sidekicks.

"You seen Shing-a-Ling?" I asked.

"Him's a changed dude," Niffty said, flicking his hands, making sure I saw his newly manicured fingernails. "Him's done changed overnight."

"What's he done?"

"Him's done gone over to the other side. Done squared-up on me and the fellows." Niffty frowned as if the words left a nasty taste on his tongue. "Him's acting like a pedigree, middle-class square."

"Where is he?"

"In the school." Niffty frowned again.

I left Niffty in the middle of the yard, still flashing his fingernails and looking pseudo-slick.

When I got to the school the class period had just ended and the halls were jammed with men, but I didn't see Shing-a-Ling anyplace.

"You seen Shing-a-Ling?" I asked the inmate clerk in the school's office.

"Yeah," the clerk said, looking up from his work, "Shing-a-Ling is in the Learning Lab."

I turned the corner and stepped into the room.

Shing-a-Ling was sitting at a study table, his head was bent forward into the learning booth and he was wearing earphones and didn't hear me walk over. For a few seconds I stood behind him reading over his shoulder and watching him flip the pages of the book and mouth the words he heard through the earphones.

"SEE DICK RUN. SEE JANE RUN. SEE DICK AND JANE RUN."

He sensed my presence, shut off the tape player, removed the earphones and looked up as he turned to me.

"Hey now LeRoy," he said. "What is it?"

"You tell me."

"Gettin' this reading thing together." He smiled.

"That's hip," I said.

"That homo done checked my game. Turned me 'round.' Did a number on me." His voice was glum, but he managed to keep a smile. "But all that's cool. I done learned a big lesson," he told me. "If a player ain't got an end game, he ain't got no game at all."

"True."

"But you can't play the game at all, 'less you can read the bulletins when they come."

"I can dig it."

"So," he said, "I'm gettin' it together."

"Solid," I said and started to leave.

"One favor?" he asked.

"Name it."

"Don't call me Shing-a-Ling any more."

I was blank.

"Call me my real name. It's nicer."

"Sure," I said, "What is it?"

"Vernon Alonzo Bowmen. It sounds square, but it's me."

I smiled for him.

He said, "Excuse my back," and put on the earphones. He turned on the tape player and went back to reading and mouthing the words as he listened. "SEE DICK RUN. SEE JANE RUN. SEE DICK AND JANE RUN."

■